What People Are Say

We see the activities of angels throughout ⸻ ⸻ ⸺aments, and they are still at work today! I know from personal ⸺ ⸻ence that God's messengers are real, that they minister to us on God's behalf—and that they are ready to come to our aid in times of crisis. In *Seeing Angels*, Joshua Mills not only describes his personal encounters with angels, but he also provides an outstanding biblical guidebook to these heavenly beings and their various roles in *all* believers' lives. You will learn to discern angels, receive God's blessings through their ministry, and work with them to further God's purposes in the world in the momentous times in which we are living. As Joshua says, "If God has a task for…angels to accomplish in our lives, I think it's important that we understand what that is." You will find that vital understanding in this book.

—*James W. Goll*
President, God Encounters Ministries
Author, *Angelic Encounters*, *The Seer*, *Strike the Mark*, and *The Discerner*

Angels are sent on assignment by God to watch over, protect, and minister to the heirs of salvation—you and me. This is a great truth. But there is so much more to these heavenly beings! In his book, *Seeing Angels*, Joshua Mills provides extensive insight and revelation into the angelic realm. He not only masterfully reveals the supporting Scripture, but also shares from his own supernatural experiences. Get ready to have the veil pulled back as you peer into the fascinating and biblical world of angels.

—*Matt Sorger*
Author and prophetic healing minister
Mattsorger.com

Let Joshua Mills mentor you about angels from firsthand experiences and deep revelation of the Scriptures. Then you won't miss the next angel you meet!

—*Sid Roth*
Host, *It's Supernatural!"*

We have great love and admiration for Joshua Mills. His pursuit and passion for the depths of God bring us great joy. We are honored to endorse his latest book, *Seeing Angels*. Joshua has a personal history of walking in congruency with the angelic realm, and therefore is equipped to share this glorious reality of heaven with you from the Bible and his own personal encounters. We encourage you to make this book one of your reference points on this important subject, especially as we are in this season the Bible refers to as the "end times." We believe *Seeing Angels* will become one of the premiere books on the ministry of angels. May it awaken your spiritual senses to discern the angelic realm and trigger personal encounters with the angelic activity all around you.

—*Mahesh and Bonnie Chavda*
Senior pastors, All Nations Church

Many years ago, God began to give me dreams, visions, and revelations of the spiritual realm, including those that revealed the work of His angels. I know from the Bible and these divine revelations that God's angels are not myths or legends. They are true spiritual beings sent to help us. I believe God inspired my friend Joshua Mills to write this book so more people will know about His kindness and goodness toward His people and His active ministry in the world. I've seen angels in action many times and can confirm what Joshua relates in *Seeing Angels*. I pray that the Lord will use this book to reach many people—bringing salvation, healing from sickness and disease, and freedom from oppression, as they learn to trust in God's Word and the power of Jesus's glorious name!

—*Dr. Mary K. Baxter*
Best-selling author, Divine Revelation series, including *A Divine Revelation of Hell*, *A Divine Revelation of Heaven*, and *A Divine Revelation of Angels*

We are on the threshold of seeing heightened angelic preser ity in the church. God sends His messengers to clear the p. through in our lives. However, we have to learn to partner with them by aligning our thoughts and words with the Word of God and declaring it in our lives. Joshua Mills's illuminating new book, *Seeing Angels*, is right on time—and on target. It demonstrates the significant ministry of angels and reveals their role in our lives so we can cooperate with their heavenly work on our behalf and also for the sake of others who urgently need a breakthrough. This book will open your eyes to the supernatural realm in which angels are being sent from God to come to your aid—today, right now!

—Dr. Kynan Bridges
Senior Pastor, Grace & Peace Global Fellowship, Tampa, FL
Author, *Invading the Heavens, Unmasking the Accuser,* and
The Power of Prophetic Prayer

Joshua Mills has created a book that is critical for the times in which we live. *Seeing Angels* is needed in the body of Christ because most Christians have no idea who angels are or what they do. Joshua dives deep into the oceans of the angelic realm and resurfaces with a book that will educate you in every aspect of angelic activity and ministry. May it provoke you to learn more about how to minister with angels.

—Andre Ashby
Founder, Souls Cry Ministries
Author, *Wild and Mighty Fire*

We are living in a time of great change, spiritual conflict, and awakening. As always, whenever God is working among mankind, angelic visitations become common. In these last days, angelic activity has greatly increased and all believers need to know how to partner with them in order to glorify God and fulfill His mission in the world. The good news is that God is raising up leaders to train and equip the body of Christ to see angels, recognize their ministry, and cooperate with them—like my good friend, Joshua Mills. Paul told Timothy to follow his example and I encourage you to follow Joshua's example. Soak in the truths of this book until they become as natural and normal for you as they are for Joshua.

—*Joan Hunter*
Author/healing evangelist, TV Host of *Miracles Happen!*

What a remarkable book! Joshua writes in such a way that we can all encounter the reality of angels in our lives. Steeped in scriptural proof, this book builds a profound understanding about angels and the realms of God, yet consistently gives all the glory to Jesus Christ *alone*. Every child of God should read this book.

—*Holly Baillie*
Spirit of God Ministries Worldwide
SpiritofGodWorldwide.com

Extraordinary! Joshua Mills has a way of making the supernatural realm tangible, real, and accessible for all. *Seeing Angels* will ignite your awareness of angels, instruct you on how to co-labor alongside them, and help guide you into your own personal experiences and encounters.

—*Robia Scott*
Actress, *Unplanned* motion picture
Author, *Counterfeit Comforts*

Joshua Mills has experienced supernatural encounters with angels and gives us not only his personal revelation, but also profound insight on angels from the Word of God in an easy-to-understand way that transports you deeper into the supernatural realm that is available for all of us. Get ready to experience the presence of God's angels in your midst.

—*Desiree Ayres*
Co-pastor, In His Presence Church, Los Angeles
Author, *God Hunger* and *Beyond the Flame*

For many years, Joshua Mills has exposed the church to unusual realms of glory and wonders. In *Seeing Angels*, he unfolds stunning revelation concerning the fascinating world of angels. For too long, too many in the church have been in the dark on this subject and missed out on so many blessings and breakthroughs. Joshua expounds on the reality and assignment of angels with profound clarity and depth. It is a teaching that will accelerate your spirit and take you to the next level of supernatural living!

—*Ryan LeStrange*
Author, *Hell's Toxic Trio*
Founder, Ryan LeStrange Ministries and the iHub Movement

Joshua Mills is clearly one of the most prolific mouthpieces and vessels that God is using in this hour to usher in His glory like never before. This book is an absolute *must read*. Joshua will take you on a journey through deep scriptural truths regarding the angelic realm, accompanied by profound experiences and encounters. Buckle up and enjoy the ride, as your life is about to be completely transformed!

—*Brian Guerin*
Founding president, Bridal Glory International

There's never been a time in human history when it has been so imperative for the body of Christ to understand and to partner with the angelic realm! And there's no better person to take you on that journey than Joshua Mills. His passionate commitment to the Word of God and the glory of God has created a firm foundation whereby the reader will not only learn about angels, but they will also be activated into a lifestyle of partnership with these wonderful divine servants. It's with great honor that I whole heartedly recommend this book to you!

—*Darren Stott*
Lead pastor, Seattle Revival Center
Founder, Supernaturalist Ministries

It has been a joy to travel the glory road with Joshua and his family for many years. I have many books about angels by noted authors on my bookshelf, but when Joshua Mills writes a book, it is a manual. In this anointed book, *Seeing Angels*, Joshua shares how he encounters angels and encourages believers to participate with the heavenly host on a daily basis. Joshua's ability to capture and share his experiences, and back them up biblically, is proof of his calling to lead us into new encounters with God. This is another tool for your "glory chest." Open our eyes, Lord!

—*Dr. Billie Reagan Deck*
Cedars of Lebanon, Inc.
ABDeck.net

I have had the unique experience of being both pastor and friend to Joshua Mills and his family since before the launch of their ministry. I am well-acquainted with the authenticity of the vehicle that God has chosen to bring this revelation through. The purpose of Joshua's ministry is to equip the church with a working knowledge of all that has been provided in Christ Jesus. *Seeing Angels* is a dynamic realm that must be fully functional in God's people today. Joshua is well-suited to be entrusted with this timely mandate.

—*D. Karl Thomas*
Senior pastor, Impact Church, London, Ontario, Canada

This book will revolutionize your spiritual life and catapult you to new heights that you may have never realized existed. The knowledge and revelation of the glory in this book contains keys to unlocking heaven on earth in your life. I have ministered with Joshua for many years. I can tell you from firsthand experience, both in ministry and in private, that he walks in the true glory of God, with signs following.

—Dr. David Herzog
TheGloryZone.org

This book brings practical insight and clarity to the realm of angels, which, at times, most everyone has had questions about. The knowledge Joshua shares is both refreshing and challenging. I would encourage anyone seeking to walk in deeper realms of the supernatural to read this book.

—Catherine Mullens
Speaker and worship artist
Catherinemullens.com

Joshua Mills has the most wonderful way of always pointing us to Jesus while sharing the supernatural realm of God! For many years, it has been a total privilege and joy to join Joshua in working with and ministering alongside angels. I have enjoyed learning so much more about these heavenly messengers through this book—and I know you will too!

—Beckah Shae
Top-10 *Billboard* chart recording artist
beckahshae.com

Seeing Angels

HOW TO RECOGNIZE AND INTERACT WITH YOUR HEAVENLY MESSENGERS

JOSHUA MILLS

WHITAKER
HOUSE

SEEING ANGELS:
How to Recognize and Interact with Your Heavenly Messengers

International Glory Ministries
P.O. Box 4037 • Palm Springs, CA 92263
JoshuaMills.com
info@joshuamills.com

ISBN: 978-1-64123-319-4 • eBook ISBN: 978-1-64123-320-0
Printed in the United States of America
© 2019 by Joshua Mills

Whitaker House • 1030 Hunt Valley Circle • New Kensington, PA 15068
www.whitakerhouse.com

Library of Congress Cataloging-in-Publication Data (Pending)

1 2 3 4 5 6 7 8 9 10 11 **LIJ** 26 25 24 23 22 21 20 19

Dedication

First, this book is dedicated to all those who have a great desire to see into the often-unseen realm. No matter how impossible it may seem to you, it really is possible. If you approach the guidance in this book with an open heart and a teachable spirit, you will begin *Seeing Angels.*

Second, this book is also dedicated to those who have eyes to see but are often misunderstood because of it. You will find your home here in this book, and a doorway to new discoveries, as the Spirit broadens your field of vision for *Seeing Angels.*

Finally, this book is also dedicated to my precious children—Lincoln, Liberty, and Legacy—for this realm must also have successors who will carry the revelation further. Read these encounters and make them your own. It is my prayer that even when you are grown up, you will still be *Seeing Angels.*

Acknowledgments

When it came time to write this book, I knew there was only one person who could help me do it in a way that would convey both the message and the impartation that needed to be shared. It was necessary to have the assistance of someone who not only understood this message, but who had also lived it. My outstanding editor, Harold McDougal, is that person. He has captured the revelation and given it voice throughout the pages of this book. Thank you for your long hours of dedication, patience, and persistence while working on this project.

Thank you also to his wife, Andrea McDougal, who assisted in the final editing process as we worked away for three days straight, finalizing everything together in New Orleans.

Thank you to Jean Albright, for doing the initial transcriptions of the many messages I've spoken all over the world, which became the initial foundation for this book.

A huge thank you to the entire family at Whitaker House: Bob Whitaker, Christine Whitaker, Don Milam, Tom Cox, Jim Armstrong, and the sales team. Also my publicity team, Karen Campbell and Judy McDonough. It is a joy working with you!

Thank you to my entire family for the way you've supported, encouraged, and blessed this project all along the way.

Thank you to my precious Miracle Worker partners with International Glory Ministries. Your monthly prayers and financial support have enabled me to carry the gospel to the nations, and for that I am truly grateful.

Finally, I must acknowledge my wife, Janet, who truly must be an earth-angel sent from heaven (either that, or a saint). In all of my travels around the world, I have never seen such patience, selfless sacrifice, and dedication to the call of God. She believes in the message we carry, and in turn, has laid down her life for it, time and time again. Only heaven will tell the story and reveal the riches of her reward. Thank you for all that you do for us, for our children, and for every person who longs to encounter the glory of God. Without *all* of your support, it would have been impossible to write this book. Because of you, many people will be *Seeing Angels*.

Contents

Foreword

Joshua Mills is not a novice when it comes to experiencing life in the spiritual dimensions and heavenly realms. He is gifted in the supernatural realm of miracles and healing, having been used by God to minister healing to hundreds of thousands of people over many years. Besides supernatural healing and miracles, there is another supernatural realm in which Joshua has had countless experiences: the realm of angelic encounters.

Seeing Angels is the result of years of study and research on the subject of angels, coupled with Joshua's own extensive, personal angelic experiences. Due to this combination of education and experience, he is more than qualified to write a book that will inform, inspire, and encourage you to open your heart and prepare yourself for your own angel encounter.

This is a needed book because it is easy for people to drift into deception regarding the subject matter. The Internet is filled with harmful material on angels that will misinform and mislead you. Joshua's grounded teaching will help you to understand the angelic realm in a much deeper way and grasp how you might safely activate angelic encounters in your own life.

Joshua will stun and stimulate you with his own angel stories. The awesome part of the book is how Joshua helps you understand how these heavenly messengers are sent to help and watch over you. You are not alone.

In closing, I will share a couple of my own experiences with angels.

In 1995, I was engaged in a prayer meeting in our home, along with many other people on our ministry team. It had been a season in which our ministry had faced some intense warfare and pressure. I was kneeling on the floor with my eyes closed. Following a prayer, I had the sense that I was to wrap up the prayer time, so I proceeded to rise from the floor. When I opened my eyes, I was shocked to see a large angel. Our living room had an open balcony that was directly above our dining room. The angel filled the space, from the dining room roof up and into the balcony. This meant that the angel was over sixteen feet tall. It was white and glistening and its face was human-like. It shocked me so much that I let out a little scream when I saw it. Unfortunately, when I screamed, it departed from sight, but to this day, I can see that angel clearly in my spirit. I will never forget it.

I asked the Lord what the purpose of the angel was, and my spirit heard Him reply, "I have sent it to battle on your behalf and to protect you." It wasn't long after that evening when our season of warfare waned.

At the time of this angelic encounter, I did not know that it was possible to be trained to discern such matters. Hebrews 5:14 says, *"But solid food is for the mature, who because of practice have their senses trained to discern both good and evil"* (NASB). You can discern the angelic realm as you *"practice"* positioning yourself to see and *"discern."* Over the years, I have done just that, and now I see angels on a regular basis, not in open vision but in my spirit. I often discern their presence by "sensing" them.

This book will raise your expectation and impart faith. God wants you to see into the unseen dimension, so get ready to activate and enter the realm of *Seeing Angels*.

—*Patricia King*
Founder, Patricia King Ministries
Cofounder, XPmedia.com

Introduction

Suddenly, an angel of the Lord appeared among them,
and the radiance of the Lord's glory surrounded them.
Luke 2:9 (NLT)

The subject of angels fascinates me, and I'm sure it does you too. Throughout history, both religious and non-religious people have witnessed the appearance of angels. I first saw them as a young child, and yet, I only became aware of their significance in my life over the past two decades. During that time, I've studied the Scriptures and spent much time in prayer, seeking God for His counsel regarding these heavenly beings. Learning how to recognize and interact with angels has been exhilarating and has kept me on the cutting edge in my ministry.

I've also had the privilege of traveling around the world to share my testimonies with others, and what I've discovered is that the more I talk about my own personal experiences with angels, the more others become aware of the presence of angels in their daily lives.

I remember, for instance, sitting in the dining room at the Cinnamon Lakeside Hotel in Colombo, Sri Lanka, several years ago. Our ministry hosts had invited some additional guests to join us. The lady across the table from me was unfamiliar with our ministry, and she asked me a simple question, "Have you ever seen an angel?"

I replied with a resounding, "Oh, yes! I see them all the time!"

My response seemed to shock her immensely. She said, "Oh, you are so blessed! I would love to see an angel."

I quickly responded by telling her, "You can! You can! You probably already have!" This excited reply seemed to shock her even more. The response of this lady was not unusual. Many people who are comfortable with the *theory* of the existence of angels seem shocked by talk of the *reality* of angels. Could this really be true? Is it really possible for humans to become aware of the angels that surround their lives on a continual basis? The answer is: Yes, it is absolutely possible!

I started to tell this lady some of my personal experiences in light of the Scriptures, and immediately she began to recollect numerous situations in which she had very likely encountered her own angels. She had been totally unaware of it until that moment. And that's exactly how it works. Many people have a deep longing to connect with the divine supernatural, but they haven't received the proper training that would enable them to make that lasting connection.

+ Do you want to learn how to see the angels God has assigned over your life?

+ Do you want to become more aware of the angelic presence that surrounds you?

+ Do you have a situation that currently needs the intervention of angels?

+ Do you want to know how to connect with these heavenly messengers, and do so in a biblical way?

If you answered "yes" to any or all of these questions, then this book is for you!

Angels Are Part of God's Plan

The Bible says that people perish when they are without vision. (See Proverbs 29:18.) I believe that seeing angels and looking into the glory realm is part of God's plan for you to succeed. Not only is it possible for you to see angels, God actually *wants* you to see them!

Although angels were created by God before the creation of the world (see Job 38:7), they are probably one of the most misunderstood parts of His design. Angels are spirit beings, and as such, they are not limited to a physical body. (See Luke 24:39.) This means that they can appear in many different forms, even taking on the appearance of humans—both male and female. (See Hebrews 13:2.) Angels are larger-than-life, unearthly beings (see Mark 8:24), sword-bearing heavenly warriors (see Numbers 22:31–35; Joshua 5:13–15), or even unusual creature-like representations (see Revelation 4:7). Through the pages of this book, I will show you biblical examples that will help you to expand your understanding and appreciation of these heavenly messengers.

Contrary to popular belief, angels sometimes have feathered wings, but at other times, they don't. Angels can also materialize in many different ways, such as through silhouette forms (see Job 4:16), flashes of light (see Ezekiel 1:14), chariot clouds (see Psalm 104:3; Daniel 7:13), rainbow colors (see Revelation 10:1), and heavenly aromas (see Revelation 8:4)—among a vast array of supernatural manifestations, and we will discuss these as well.

God never does anything by accident, and He certainly doesn't place an angel in your life without a divine purpose. If God has a task for these angels to accomplish in our lives, I think it's important that we understand what that is.

Are [angels] *not all ministering spirits, sent forth to minister for them who shall be heirs of salvation?* (Hebrews 1:14)

The Scriptures tell us that they have been commissioned to our lives as heavenly messengers or *"ministering spirits"* who serve the purposes of God for us. But success in their appointed tasks requires cooperation on our part.

I have met my angels, I understand their purpose, and I am aware of their presence as I minister around the world. I work with them on a regular basis and am continually meeting new angels who are being released to carry out new tasks all around me.

I believe that you can also recognize and interact with your angels, and that you should. I want to help you understand this heavenly realm. Many students who have attended my spiritual training seminars and schools have reported having an increased awareness of the angelic activity taking place around them. Therefore, I will also teach you these spiritual practices I have learned that have enabled me to become much more sensitive to angelic realities. Keep your heart open and your spirit ready to receive instruction from the Word of God.

I will be sharing some of my own personal testimonies with you, but this is not just a testimony book. This is a guidebook that will help you increase your awareness of angels. In turn, you will be able to share your personal angelic testimonies with others.

In this book, I have prepared activations and prayers along with the teachings. Please take time not only to read the book, but also to be intentional about interacting with the revelation. When I released my last book, *Moving in Glory Realms*,[1] many people heard the Spirit telling them: "Read it slowly, take your time, because there is an encounter waiting for you within its pages," and I believe it will be the same with this book. And the results will be phenomenal. Don't feel rushed or pressured by the information you receive. Instead, find a spiritual rhythm that will carry you through it in a peaceful way. I am excited to hear about the end results—what you see, hear, and discover regarding the angels that surround your life.

Finally, the most important thing to remember as we delve into this supernatural subject, is that Jesus Christ is higher than the angels. (See Hebrews 1:4.) Jesus is Lord! We don't worship, pray to, or bow down to any angel. Our only desire in pursuing this realm is that Jesus Christ might be lifted up and exalted in our lives in a more vibrant way.

Although the topic and title of this book is *Seeing Angels*, my desire is that you would ultimately see Jesus Christ surrounding your life with His loving care and concern. God has given us access to the angels because He loves us dearly. My prayer is that you would know God's love, experience His love, and embrace His love through developing a healthy and authentic

---

1. Joshua Mills, *Moving in Glory Realms: Exploring Dimensions of Divine Presence* (New Kensington, PA: Whitaker House, 2018).

relationship with Jesus Christ. He is the Commander of the hosts of angels, and you will not be able to properly connect with them, or with Him, until you allow Jesus to be the Lord of your life. If you've never invited Him into your heart to be your personal Lord and Savior, why not pray this prayer now:

Jesus, come into my heart. I invite You to be my Lord and Savior. I give You my sin in exchange for the life that only You can give. Thank You for cleansing me with Your blood and giving me a brand-new start. I receive Your gift of salvation. Amen!

If you've just prayed that prayer by faith, you can be sure that Jesus now lives in your heart, and He will begin to help you in your spiritual journey.

Angels enhance our usefulness for God's service, and I am thankful for the angels who God has allowed me to work with. The result has been that millions of people around the world have heard the gospel message preached and have seen the evidence of that message demonstrated through signs, wonders, and miracles. In the process, my life has been blessed in countless ways.

If you're ready to start *Seeing Angels*, let's pray:

Father, in the name of Jesus, I desire to be more effective in Your kingdom work. I know that You have assigned Your angels over my life, and I want to become more aware of this angelic realm that You have provided for me. Thank You for helping me to find my pace in the rhythm of Your glory, as I give myself to focus, read, and expand my understanding through this book. Jesus, I give You first place in my life. I give You permission to correct, redirect, or clarify any misunderstandings I might have about angels. Holy Spirit, I invite You to teach and lead me into all truth. Thank You for increasing my sensitivity to Your Spirit as I study Your Word and search out Your ways. In Jesus's holy name, amen!

PART I

Understanding Your Angels

"Believers, look up—take courage.
The angels are nearer than you think."
—*Billy Graham*

1

Angels in Your Life

For He shall give His angels charge over you,
to keep you in all your ways.
Psalm 91:11

Angels are real. I have angels assigned to my life, and you do too! Every believer has angels commissioned to them, to perform certain specific tasks to which they are called. Some angels bring healing, while others deliver important messages, and, as we can see throughout the Scriptures, there are many angels committed to the protection and deliverance of God's people. (See, for example, Psalm 34:7.) The most important thing to remember is that there are specific angels assigned to *you*. Whether you've noticed them or not doesn't change this reality. From the beginning of history, the activity of angels has been documented within the Word of God, and every place where an angel is mentioned in the Bible represents an area of your own life where an angel is available to work for you!

In this first chapter, I want you to see the various classifications of angels that are recorded in the Bible. I've also provided an appendix filled with Scripture to enhance your understanding of this topic. I want you to have the confidence to know that angels are present with you, that they have been sent by God, and that they are waiting for you to engage with them, today and every day!

The Hebrew word translated as *angel* in the Bible is *mal'ak* (Strong's H4397), which means "messenger from God," "ambassador," or "to dispatch as a deputy." The Greek word *aggelos* carries a similar meaning, denoting a "messenger" or "sent one." Although you may not always see your angels, according to God's Word, you can be sure that your angels always see you! They are heavenly messengers being sent to positively affect your life. They surround you constantly, whether you're aware of their presence or not. Most of us have only been taught about the physical realm that surrounds us in time and space, but there is a much wider spiritual realm that penetrates the natural world with the vibrations of the eternal. The existence of angels reminds us that a reality exists far beyond that which we can see in the natural, and one of the reasons I have written this book is to help you become more aware of these angelic beings. Yes, *beings*, plural. The Scriptures say that you have more than one of them: *"For he shall give His angels charge over you"*!

ALTHOUGH YOU MAY NOT ALWAYS SEE YOUR ANGELS, ACCORDING TO GOD'S WORD, YOU CAN BE SURE THAT YOUR ANGELS ALWAYS SEE YOU!

When I was very young, I used to play with my angels in the backyard, swinging with them on the playset and singing songs with them. I even remember watching angels flying in circles above my head in church, gliding through the air with ease beneath the ceiling of the sanctuary during our Sunday morning services. They were dressed in what seemed to be white, flowing gowns, and they radiated the most brilliant light as they flew gracefully through the air.

There were usually more than one of them, and I find it interesting that when the Scriptures speak of angels, they are often mentioned in groups. Angels seem to love to work together to accomplish God's purposes in the earth. In large numbers and by many names, we can see various angels mentioned in the Bible. They have been called:

+ The armies of heaven (Revelation 19:14)

+ Chariots of fire (2 Kings 6:17; see also Psalm 68:17; Zechariah 6:1–5)

+ Heavenly hosts (Psalms 103:21, 148:2; Luke 2:13)

+ Holy ones (Psalm 89:5 and 7)

+ An innumerable company (Hebrews 12:22)

+ Sons of God (Job 1:6 and 2:1)

+ Stars (Job 38:7; Revelation 12:4)

+ Watchers (Daniel 4:13, 17)

When we read these descriptive names of God's angels, such as *"chariots of fire," "heavenly hosts,"* and *"stars,"* immediately, we think of bright shining lights, and that would be true. Someone has said, "Angels are to God what sunbeams are to the sun." This is correct in the sense that angels come from God and are an extension of Him, and in the sense that they release His heavenly radiance in the earth. However, I don't want you to be confused about angels, so I feel the need to clarify certain truths up front, in order to help you get your mind properly focused on what I'm referring to in this book.

Who Is *"the Angel of the Lord"*?

One of the things that has puzzled biblical scholars and theologians for centuries is the use of the term *"the angel of the Lord"* throughout the Scriptures. On a few occasions in the Old Testament, this could have been Jesus Himself, appearing in Spirit form. This is called a *theophany*, a manifestation or appearance of the pre-incarnate Christ. This would explain the angel's authority to forgive sins (see Exodus 23:21), judge the earth (see Genesis 18:25), and receive worship from both Moses and Joshua (see Exodus 3:2–5; Joshua 5:14–15), for these are things that only God can do. We should, however, be careful to understand that this does not mean that Jesus is merely an angel. He is higher than the angels (see Hebrews 1:4), He is the one and only Son of God (see Hebrews 1:1–5), the angels worship

Him (see Hebrews 1:6–7), and whereas angels are created heavenly beings (see Psalm 148:1–6), we know that Jesus has existed for all of eternity (see John 1:1–14).

We also see the angel of the Lord appearing in New Testament times. A good example is when the angel of the Lord appeared to Joseph, foretelling the birth of Christ:

> *But while he thought on these things, behold, the angel of the Lord appeared to him in a dream, saying, Joseph, you son of David, fear not to take to you Mary your wife: for that which is conceived in her is of the Holy Ghost. And she shall bring forth a son, and you shall call His name* JESUS: *for He shall save His people from their sins.*
>
> (Matthew 1:20–21)

This angel's identity is not completely revealed in that passage, but Luke wrote about the angel Gabriel visiting Zacharias and Mary. (See Luke 1:11–20, 26–37.) On two other occasions when the angel of the Lord appeared to Joseph, Jesus had already been born. It wouldn't make sense to think that Jesus could be both the young child and the angel at the same time. In other New Testament Scriptures, the angel of the Lord helped Peter to escape from prison (see Acts 12:7) and struck down King Herod (see Acts 12:23). While we can conclude with certainty that in some instances, the angel of the Lord was God Himself, in most other occurrences, this angel was merely another of the ministering spirits sent forth from the Lord.

The late famed evangelist Billy Graham wrote:

> …in some cases in the Old Testament, God Himself appeared in human form as an angel. This reinforces the idea of the relationship between God and His angels. Nevertheless, in almost all of the cases where angelic personages appear, they are God's created angelic beings and not God Himself.[2]

---

2. Billy Graham, *Angels: God's Secret Agents* (Nashville, TN: W Publishing Group, 1994), 31.

What we do know for certain is that the same angels of the Lord who moved and ministered in the lives of the ancients are still a part of the heavenly host, and they are ready to minister to us and for us today.

All of God's Angels Praise Him

The angels we will be looking at in this book are *not* God, and God is *not* an angel. Angels are created beings. (See Colossians 1:16.) God created them even before He created the earth, for the Scriptures tell us that the angels sang at creation:

> *Where were you when I laid the foundations of the earth? declare, if you have understanding. Who has laid the measures thereof, if you know? or who has stretched the line upon it? Whereupon are the foundations thereof fastened? or who laid the corner stone thereof; when the morning stars sang together, and all the sons of God shouted for joy?*
>
> (Job 38:4–7)

Angels were created to sing God's praises, so we should never worship an angel. Instead, we should join with them in giving all glory to God Almighty Himself.

The angels I was aware of as a child were always giving glory to God. When they appeared in our backyard, we spent hours singing together. My singing was sometimes so loud that our next-door neighbor commented about it to my mother, saying that he rather enjoyed the sound of my music filling his yard. This happened on more than one occasion.

The Wings of Angels

As I watched angels flying beneath the ceiling of the church sanctuary, it seemed as though even their flight was somehow an expression of praise. I don't remember seeing wings on those particular angels, but that didn't seem to hinder them from soaring about in a supernatural way. Some angels have wings, while others do not. Some have two wings, some have four wings (see Ezekiel 1:6), and some have six wings. Those extra wings cover their face, hands, and feet. (See Isaiah 6:2.)

When I was a child, one of my guardian angels had what appeared to be oversized butterfly-type wings that glowed with a blueish hue. I've seen angels that had large and broad wings like an eagle and others that had thin, delicate wings that appeared to be a part of their garments in some way. Last summer when I was preaching in Virginia, I saw an angel appear amongst the people there. His entire being seemed to be dancing with a mother-of-pearl shimmer, his wings being an integral part of him.

WITHOUT JESUS, THERE IS NO GLORY; WITH JESUS, THERE IS GLORY EVERYWHERE.

The wings of some cherubim are awesome in appearance because they have eyes within those wings. The closest thing on earth I could compare this to would be a peacock feather, but even that doesn't give you the full picture. I first saw a glimpse of these creatures with their wings and their eyes many years ago, while ministering at the home Bible study of my friends Earl and Lynda Stroud in Genoa, Illinois. There were only a handful of us gathered together that night in their basement, but the Bible promises us, *"where two or three are gathered together in My name, there am I in the midst of them"* (Matthew 18:20). Without Jesus, there is no glory; with Jesus, there is glory everywhere, and when the glory comes, it brings a realm of seeing. As we were worshipping the Lord, suddenly these creatures seemed to flash across my field of vision. I could see that the feathers were the eyes, and the eyes were the feathers, layer upon layer.

Holy Angels Reflect God's Glory

Angels carry the life essence of God and reflect His glory. They do not bring glory to themselves, but, rather, direct all glory to Jesus. For example, consider the mighty angelic creatures that Ezekiel saw. Although they were a mysterious form of spiritual being, the Bible tells us clearly that they had four faces:

> *As for the likeness of their faces, they four had the face of a man, and the face of a lion, on the right side: and they four had the face of an ox on the left side; they four also had the face of an eagle.* (Ezekiel 1:10)

- *"The face of a man"* reflects the person of Jesus, who was the Word made flesh and became man for our sake. (See John 1:14.)
- *"The face of a lion"* reveals the kingly authority of Jesus, the Lion of Judah that roars with victory. (See Numbers 24:9; Revelation 5:5.)
- *"The face of an ox"* represents ultimate sacrifice. During Old Testament times, the ox was the most costly of sacrifices. Jesus came to earth as a servant, to sacrifice Himself, so that we might find eternal life through Him. (See Matthew 20:28; Mark 10:43).
- *"The face of an eagle"* radiates the prophetic revelation that Jesus Christ has risen to the highest heights with resurrection glory, taking dominion over all spiritual principalities and powers. (See Ephesians 2:6; Colossians 2:15.)

When we look upon these mighty angelic creatures, all we can see is the revelation of Jesus Christ. All of God's heavenly beings were created to bring Him glory and reflect His glory!

Are Angels Male or Female?

An angel is a pure spirit, in that it has no physical matter. Angels are spirit beings with personal spirit bodies. Martin Luther wrote, "An angel is a spiritual creature created by God without a body, for the service of Christendom and of the church."[3] If they choose to manifest in physical form, they can do so, but they are not limited by that physical form. Most often, in the Scriptures, we see angels mentioned as being male, but, again, since they are spirit beings, according to Scripture, they are without gender.

Gender is a biological function, and since angels do not have a biological function, there is no reason for them to have a specific gender identity.

---

3. Martin Luther, *Table Talk* (1566).

(See Matthew 22:30.) It is possible for an angel to manifest in either male or female form, and the way God allows them to present themselves often speaks of their spiritual assignment on earth. In general, the male gender is associated with aggression, strength, and authority, whereas the female gender is associated with nurture, love, and wisdom.

The grammatical gender of the Hebrew word *ruach* (which means "spirit") is feminine. So is the feminine word *shekinah* in rabbinic literature, which indicates "the visible glory of God." The book of Proverbs references a spirit that many biblical scholars refer to as "Lady Wisdom" (see Proverbs 1:20–22; 8:1–9:3), and we see the two female angels in Zechariah 5:9, who are working for God. So, from this biblical evidence, we can conclude that there are both male and female representations in the spirit world, which needs to be understood metaphorically rather than physically, because, again, spirit beings are pure spirit.

Different Types of Angels Mentioned in the Bible

When these heavenly beings circle around God's throne, I can tell you that they have greater vision of His majesty than anything we could ever imagine. And I believe that's part of the reason they come when we worship: to help us understand just how holy, magnificent, and awesome the Lord is! Actually, if we look at all the angels that God has created in the glory realms, we can glean a vision of the way things work.

In the history of Christianity, several theologians have set out to understand the celestial hierarchy by focusing on four specific passages of Scripture[4] in order to develop an arrangement of three spheres, each one containing three orders of angels. Although the biblical canon is relatively silent on this subject, we know for sure that these heavenly beings differ in power, some having authority that others don't possess. There are certainly ranks of angels, and I think the idea is worth noting here as we set out to explore the different types of angels mentioned specifically within the pages of the Bible. If you've read my book, *Moving in Glory Realms*, you'll recognize that each one of these celestial spheres corresponds with both a spiritual realm and a heavenly realm.

---

4. Galatians 3:26–28; Matthew 22:24–33; Ephesians 1:21–23; Colossians 1:16

Three Celestial Spheres and the Nine Orders of Angels

Jesus Christ

After he finished the sacrifice for sins, the Son took his honored place high in the heavens right alongside God, far higher than any angel in rank and rule. Did God ever say to an angel, "You're my Son; today I celebrate you" or "I'm his Father, he's my Son"? When he presents his honored Son to the world, he says, "All angels must worship him."

(Hebrews 1:3–6 MSG)

First Celestial Sphere The highest heaven: the third heavenly dimension Psalm 115:16	◆ Psalm 104:4; Isaiah 6:1–7 ◆ Genesis 3:24; Exodus 25:18–21; Ezekiel 10:14 ◆ Ezekiel 10:17; Daniel 7:9; Colossians 1:16	◆ Seraphim ◆ Cherubim ◆ Thrones
Second Celestial Sphere The cosmic heaven: the second heavenly dimension Revelation 14:6	◆ Ephesians 1:21; Colossians 1:16 ◆ Ephesians 1:21 ◆ Ephesians 3:10, 6:12; 2 Thessalonians 1:7	◆ Dominions ◆ Virtues ◆ Powers
Third Celestial Sphere The lower heaven: the first heavenly dimension Revelation 21:1	◆ Ephesians 1:21, 3:10 ◆ Jude 1:9; 1 Thessalonians 4:16 ◆ Psalm 34:7; Luke 22:43; Hebrews 1:14, 13:2	◆ Principalities ◆ Archangels ◆ Ministering Spirits

One thing you'll notice about my chart is that I always include Jesus in any conversation about angels because He is God, and everything directs back to Him. We must make sure that we keep things in proper perspective, especially when dealing with spiritual realities. Jesus is higher than all the angels—higher in power, authority, and lordship. He is Lord over all!

Let's continue to examine the various orders of angels that God has created, to understand their interaction with the earth and their intended purpose for existence. The angels in the first celestial sphere, are those that abide continuously in the third heaven dimension.

Seraphim

The Scriptures speak about a class of angels called *seraphim*. They are filled with fire and blazing light. *Seraph* is singular, while *seraphim* is the plural form. Their name means "the burning ones." They are flaming angels that emanate such bright light no one can look upon them. As amazing as this is, we should remember that essentially all angels are "light beings." St. Augustine believed that all of God's angels were created in the very moment when God said, "Let there be light!" (Genesis 1:3).[5]

Seraphim have six wings each, two covering their feet, two covering their face, and two utilized for flight. It was a seraph who touched Isaiah's lips with a burning coal from the altar, cleansing him from sin. (See Isaiah 6:1–7.) The seraphim serve as attendants and caretakers at God's throne and are involved in continuous worship, singing the Hebrew Kadosh—"Holy, holy, holy is the Lord of Hosts!" When we sing this Jewish prayer, we join in the song that's continuously being sung in heaven.

Cherubim

Cherubim, another type of angel, are God's celestial attendants. *Cherub* is the singular, while *cherubim* is the plural. Their name means "the fullness of wisdom." They are an order of angels with wings that guard the holiness of God's light and His glory. Although the four living creatures from Revelation, with beastly appearance and six wings, are in this order of angels, they are usually man-like in appearance. The cherubim are winged

---

5. St. Augustine, *The City of God*, chapter 9 (A.D. 426).

protectors of God's throne. The image of this angel was placed upon the ark of the covenant as a symbolic representation of their being guardians of the glory.

Thrones

These angels represent the steadfast love of God and the dynamic interaction of His holy purposes. Sometimes called Ophanim, they appear as flaming, moving wheels covered with eyes. (See Daniel 7:8–9; Ezekiel 1:15–21.) They are living symbols of God's judgment, power, and authority. Along with the Seraphim and Cherubim, they guard the throne of God's glory.

The orders of angels in the second sphere are involved in organization. They are concerned with the way things function on a universal scale.

Dominions

Dominions are angels of leadership. They govern the universe and are ministers of divine order. Dominions are known for delivering God's justice into unjust situations, and also for showing mercy toward human beings. They regulate the duties of lower-ranking angels, making known the commands of God.

Virtues

This name *virtue* is more commonly translated as "heavenly authorities." According to the dictionary, the word *authority* means "the power or right to give orders, make decisions, and enforce obedience," and that's exactly what these angels do. The virtues work to encourage people and motivate them toward making wise choices, choices of faith. They offer supernatural strength and divine energy when needed.

Powers

These are warrior angels who wage war against demonic powers. They are in a continuous battle against the forces of evil in the second-heaven dimension, holding back wicked enemy strategies, attacks, and assignments plotted against God's people.

The orders of angels in the third sphere are much more involved in the day-to-day functions of life here on earth.

Principalities

These angels are assigned to watch over and care for specific communities, regional states, and kingdoms. Often, they are associated with transitions in power and are charged with fulfilling the divine ministry within the borders of a set region. These are the angels who preside over nations and are said to inspire many things, such as art, science, and culture.

Principalities are physically differentiated from other angels by the crowns they wear and the scepters they carry. Sometimes, they are dressed in the garments of the nations they represent. In describing them, the apostle Paul used the terms *"rule and authority"* in Ephesians 1:21 (NIV) and *"rulers and authorities"* in Ephesians 3:10 (NIV).

Archangels

These are the chief angels who are assigned to communicate and carry out God's specific plans for mankind. Michael is the only archangel mentioned specifically by name in the Bible. (See Jude 1:9.) However, because the Scriptures tell us that Gabriel stands in the presence of God (see Luke 1:19), it is believed that he and the other angels mentioned in Revelation 8:2 could also be archangels. Some Christian traditions go so far as to recognize the other five by specific names.[6] But this is just speculation, since our biblical canon doesn't provide this specific information.

Some have taught that it is important to call on the name of an archangel when needing assistance. This is a wrong teaching that can lead to error and a form of angel worship. The apostle Paul warned us specifically against this in Colossians 2:18: *"Let no man beguile you of your reward in a voluntary humility and **worshiping of angels**."* Instead, always call on the name of Jesus Christ, knowing that through Him, God has given His angels charge over you!

Ministering Spirits

---

6. See the Apocryphal books of Tobit and Enoch.

Ministering spirits are the angels we interact with the most. They are the angels who work continually in the material world, abiding within the first heaven and carrying out God's orders among us. Our guardian angels—angels of protection, support, deliverance, miracles, and healing—are among this classification. (See Luke 22:43; Hebrews 1:14, 13:2.)

AS I BEGIN *SEEING ANGELS*, I WILL KEEP MY FOCUS ON ALL THAT GOD HAS COMMANDED ME TO DO!

Each class of angelic being is different from the other, and they all serve their own individual purposes in the eternal plan of God. As you prepare to begin *Seeing Angels*, I want you to make the following declaration with me. Say it out loud, and allow the words of it to begin resonating within your spirit:

> I can see angels in the Bible, because God has given them a place, plan, and purpose in the Scriptures!
>
> I can also see angels in my life, because God has given them a place, a plan, and a purpose for me!
>
> The angels follow God's precepts, as they point me toward Jesus Christ!
>
> I follow God's precepts, as I point others toward Jesus Christ!
>
> As I begin Seeing Angels, I will keep my focus on all that God has commanded me to do!

You may want to copy this declaration and put it where you can see it every day. Make this bold statement on a daily basis!

2

Angels of Protection, Deliverance, and Comfort

My God sent his angel, and he shut the mouths of the lions.
They have not hurt me, because I was found innocent in his sight.
Daniel 6:22 (NIV)

God has given us angels of protection and deliverance, just as He did for Daniel. When His servant needed supernatural protection, God knew just what to do. He could have come down from heaven and shut the lions' mouths Himself. His hand is big enough to shut more than one lion's mouth at a time. Certainly God is all-powerful and He could have shut all of them—but He didn't.

Why didn't He come down from His heavenly throne to shut the lions' mouths?

On the other hand, why should a king get off of his throne when he has plenty of attendants to do his bidding?

God has His holy angels to do whatever He desires for them to do. (See Hebrews 1:14.) Kings decree and declare, but then their servants carry out those decrees and declarations. Likewise, God gives the instructions, and the angels hear those instructions and rush to carry them out. When

God's Word is spoken, angels take notice. They are attentive to His Word, and when they hear it, they begin to move immediately and do whatever is necessary to fulfill it.

In the case of Daniel, his protective angels had to enter the den and close the mouths of the lions so they would not harm Daniel—and the angels did just that.

Angels of protection are available in your life too. When do they come? When they hear God's words spoken. That's what sets them in motion. You might think you have been waiting on angels like that, but the truth is, they have been waiting on you! They move at the voice of their King.

Psalm 103:20 also declares this truth:

Praise the Lord, *you his angels, you mighty ones who do his bidding, who obey his word.* (NIV)

Angels are just waiting to "*do his bidding*," and "*obey his word.*" But how is God's Word heard these days in the earth? Is it not through you and me? As the children of God and the heirs of salvation, we now have that responsibility. The Scriptures tell us that our Lord "*has made us kings and priests to God and His Father; to Him be glory and dominion for ever and ever. Amen*" (Revelation 1:6). It is now our responsibility to speak, to give voice to God's Word in the earth. As we do that, angels obey and begin to act in accordance with what has been spoken.

If you need an angel of protection to show up in your life, now you know what you need to do to bring it to pass. Speak God's Word of protection (and there are many Scriptures to be found on that subject in your Bible). As an exercise, look up some verses that promise God's protection. When you find them, speak what they promise, and thereby activate angels to work on your behalf. You will be pleasantly surprised.

Unusual Angels in the Arctic

A few years ago, my wife, Janet, and I received a phone call from our dear friend Louisa, who lives in a place called Quaqtaq, far north in the Canadian Arctic.

It was wintertime, and Louisa was calling out of desperation because her husband, Johnny, who had been mayor of that community for many terms, had gone hunting with his son, Alec, on their snowmobiles. They had taken some supplies along and were planning to be gone for a while, but, without warning, an arctic blizzard had overtaken them and their lives were now at grave risk.

It is difficult for most of us to understand such a situation. For one thing, we don't get such terrible winter storms where we live, and second, we always have supply stores nearby when we do. In the Arctic, when you're traveling between communities, it's just you and the land. Many of the Inuit people have modern means of communication, but even those have their limits.

The people of Quaqtaq had lost contact with Johnny and Alec and were no longer sure exactly where they were located. Louisa was asking for prayer.

Janet and I prayed with Louisa, and as we were praying, the Lord urged us to begin speaking His Word and commanding angels to be activated on assignment in this desperate situation. Even though we were in southern Canada and Johnny and Alec were far away in northern Canada, that didn't matter to God. Time and space are irrelevant with Him. When you speak God's words, something begins to happen. Angels love the Word of God. They agree with it and move according to its decree. The more we speak God's words (and *really* believe them as we do) the more we will see angels moving on our behalf.

WHEN GOD'S WORD BECOMES ALIVE TO US,
WE WILL BECOME ALIVE WITH THE WORD AND
ACTIVATE ANGELS ALL AROUND US!

In his book, *Angels on Assignment*, Rolland Buck shared that the angel Gabriel spoke to him, saying, "Read the Word; feed on it; let it become the living Word to you, not just columns of truths and opinions of men."[7] When God's Word becomes alive to us, we will become alive with the Word and activate angels all around us!

As Janet and I spoke God's promises over Johnny and Alec, we could sense that angels were being released and going forth on their assignments. We went on social media and asked our followers to speak God's Word and activate angels on behalf of Johnny and Alec as well. Even if they were lost somewhere in the Arctic, God knew exactly where they were.

Several days passed before we received the report that Johnny and Alec had been rescued and brought to safety. This was an answer to our prayers. We were sure it was a great miracle, but we didn't know the details until several months later when we were able to visit them. How wonderful it was to greet Johnny, Louisa, Alec, and their family. And what a wonderful story Johnny told us!

He said that when the storm first overtook them, they got out a tarp they had taken with them, fastened it between the two snowmobiles, and huddled together beneath it. That, however, didn't provide much shelter. Snow was blowing in under the tarp and the cold was debilitating.

As Inuit people of the Arctic, they knew how to exist in this kind of weather, but they hadn't been prepared for the harshness of this storm, so they had not packed enough supplies for a proper shelter. In time, the cold sapped their strength. Johnny knew that this was one of the last phases of hypothermia, before you fall asleep and never wake up again. They prayed together and felt assured that they were ready for heaven.

Just as their last bit of strength was fading and their eyes were beginning to close, they heard a man and a woman talking. The woman seemed to be Swedish and the man looked to be Hispanic. And they just appeared out of nowhere in the Canadian Arctic. There were no roads nearby. No normal vehicle could have reached them. The only way to travel around was by snowmobile or dogsled, and yet, a Swedish woman and an Hispanic

---

7. Roland Buck, *Angels on Assignment* (New Kensington, PA: Whitaker House, 2005), 41.

man had suddenly appeared on foot, shouting, "Wake up! Wake up! You can't go to sleep!"

This roused Johnny and Alec enough to begin having a conversation with this couple. Johnny later said it was the strangest conversation he'd ever had, and in the midst of it, he kept trying to figure out how these people had gotten there in the first place. But the ongoing conversation, which, in hindsight, didn't seem to make much sense, served its purpose—it kept them awake.

How long this went on, the two men could not say. All they knew was that it kept them awake long enough for a search team to discover Johnny and Alec wide awake, not sleeping. They were alive, not dead. What a miracle!

As the search team arrived, the foreigners wandered off. Some might conjecture that a Swedish woman and an Hispanic man just happened to be wandering around the wilderness of the Canadian Arctic that day, and I guess it is naturally possible (although highly unlikely and extremely unusual). But I firmly believe that man and woman were angels sent by God with the purpose of keeping those two men awake so that they would live. That's what angels of protection do.

God has angels of protection for you too. When they come, they may come in some of the most extraordinary, unusual, and uncommon ways, but don't be guilty of quickly dismissing their ministry. We have sometimes thought that an angel must look a certain way or act a certain way, but they can come in all shapes and sizes, taking on the appearance of any gender or nationality. I've met angels who seemed to be Asian, Brazilian, African-American, Middle Eastern, or some other nationality.

An Angel Saved My Daughter from Harm

As you fill your home with God's Word, you'll fill your life with God's angels. Sometimes we require the ministry of angels without advance warning, or without us even being aware of our need. This happened to me not too long ago.

I wasn't feeling very well one day and had gone to bed and fallen asleep. Janet needed to take our son to work, so she woke me up and told me that she was leaving, and that our young daughters, Liberty and Legacy, were going to stay home with me. They were playing together in their bedroom. I went back to sleep.

AS YOU FILL YOUR HOME WITH GOD'S WORD, YOU'LL FILL YOUR LIFE WITH GOD'S ANGELS.

Suddenly, I was awakened by someone whispering in my ear. A voice I didn't recognize was saying, "Cece! Cece!" (Cece is our nickname for our three-year-old, Legacy.) Why was I hearing her name being spoken? Who was speaking? I lifted my head and looked around, but there was no one else in the room. Feeling a sense of urgency, I got up quickly and ran across the hallway into the girls' room. Liberty was sitting on the floor playing with some toys, and I asked her, "Where is Cece?" She said she didn't know.

I ran back out into the hallway and called her name, "Cece!" But there was no response.

Together, Liberty and I called Cece's name throughout the rest of the upstairs. Again there was no response.

We went downstairs and saw that the front door had been left open. It was the beginning of winter, the temperature outside was freezing cold, and it didn't make any sense that the door had been left open. Had Cece opened the door and wandered outside for some reason? Now our search took on increased urgency.

I yelled out the door, "Cece! Cece!" Still, there was no response.

I scrambled to put on a pair of shoes and a winter jacket and ran out on the driveway calling her name. Suddenly, there she was, walking calmly down the street with her cute little face, wearing only a nightgown and a pair of boots. The frigid roads were covered with ice and snow. I ran to her and swept her up into my arms, sure that an angel of protection had awakened me so that I could find her before anything happened to her.

To this day, I still don't know how long Cece was outside in the cold. She said she had gone looking for her mommy, who, of course, had left home already. In her innocence, she didn't realize that she had put her life in such danger. Thank God, He had His angels watching over us.

There are angels available to protect your family members and loved ones. There are angels available to protect your peace. There are angels available to protect your possessions and property. There are angels available to protect your finances and inheritance. There are angels available to protect your ministry and guard the anointing on your life. God has angels of protection for you.

Angels of Comfort

Several times in my life, I have felt God send His angels to comfort me in difficult situations. At times, as I have prayed to the Lord, I've felt a gentle, affirming hand resting on my shoulder or touching my back. Have you ever felt that?

Recently, while I was getting my hair cut, my hairdresser and I got into a conversation. I told her that I was writing a book about seeing angels. She excitedly exclaimed, "Oh, I have a story! And most people would never understand it."

I told her that I wanted to hear the story, and this is what she told me:

Many years ago, I was in a great deal of pain, and the doctors found a small, pea-sized tumor on one of my kidneys. They were greatly concerned, so they booked me for a further CT scan. The waitlist to have that test was two months long, and by the time I got the scan, the tumor had already grown to the size of a golf ball. It was two weeks before Christmas, and this was not the news we had hoped to hear.

My husband sat beside me in that hospital room and held both of my hands in his. My head was down, and I was trying to understand what something like this would mean. Then, suddenly, I felt two large arms being wrapped around me from behind in a sort of bear hug. I imagined, at first, that it was my husband and I tried to imagine how he could be hugging me in this way, but I quickly realized that I was still holding his hands, so it couldn't have been him.

In that moment, a great sense of peace washed over me, and I immediately knew that everything was going to be all right. My angel had come to bring me comfort during one of the most emotionally challenging days of my life. That was twenty-three years ago, and I have never forgotten it!

She went on to explain that although there had still been a few bumps in the road, she had held on to the memory of that hug, and the fact that she knew it was a divine moment. And that memory carried her through it all.

God doesn't promise us that we won't have problems in our lives. In fact, we are guaranteed to face some difficult situations and hard decisions. What we *are* promised is that His angels will always be there with us. During good times, these angels will help keep us balanced, so we don't fall into pride. During bad times, they will help us navigate the path set before us with wisdom and grace, always reminding us of God's promises.

Angels Can Help Relieve Your Stress

During times of intense pressure, our angels come to alleviate the stress and strengthen us to be faithful in our commitments and responsibilities. When sudden disruptions attempt to derail our lives, there are angels who come to bring recovery, ministering God's blessing.

In Isaiah 40:1, God is speaking to His angels and commanding them: *"Comfort, comfort my people"* (NLT). This is one of the assignments God gives His angels to perform. I recently heard someone describe the feeling that their angel was leaning on their shoulder. Others have said they commonly feel a gentle "pat of approval" on the back of their head, or an invisible arm that seems to wrap around their side. You will feel a calming presence when God's angels come, as they bring a peaceful shift to any stressful or overwhelming situation.

Although many people are not aware of their angel's physical presence, they still testify to sensing their presence spiritually. They often describe the experience as "a heavy load being lifted off of my shoulders." Stress and spiritual heaviness are the work of the enemy, and they play a part in the onset of headaches, high blood pressure, heart problems, diabetes, skin conditions, asthma, arthritis, depression, and anxiety. When God's angels arrive, they shift the atmosphere from one of tension and anxiety into one of peace and heavenly tranquility.

Right now, I want you to close your eyes and take a deep breath. Then, with your eyes closed, I want you to picture two large angels standing beside you, ministering God's comfort to you. This is biblical. Psalm 91:11 says, *"He shall give His angels charge over you, to keep you in all your ways."* You have at least two angels watching over you, guarding you, and ministering God's comfort to you at all times.

Your desire for *Seeing Angels* is scriptural, and God wants to make these angels of protection, deliverance, and comfort a reality for you. Let's pray together to that end. If you're ready to start *Seeing Angels*, let's pray:

> Father, in the name of Jesus, Your Word says that You are faithful, and that You will strengthen me and protect me from the evil one.[8] Right now, I thank You for releasing Your angels of protection over my life. I take comfort in Your Word, and I find my refuge in You. Although I may have many troubles, I know that You are delivering me from all of them.[9] I know that You are spreading Your protection over me,[10] as Your angels surround my life. I trust You, and I will rest in Your safety. In Jesus's precious name, amen!

---

8. 2 Thessalonians 3:3.
9. Psalm 34:19.
10. Psalm 5:11.

3

Angels of Healing

*For an angel went down at a certain season into the pool,
and troubled the water: whosoever then first after the troubling of the
water stepped in was made whole of whatsoever disease he had.*
John 5:4

God has angels of healing available for you. These are angels who move between heaven and earth to bring forth the manifestation of healing in our lives. They come into our homes, workplaces, schools, and ministries, bringing gifts of healing and miracles of all kinds.

These angels heal anything—defective organs, damaged tissue, deficient blood cells, degenerated bones, strained and torn muscles—you name it. Nothing is too difficult for God, and no health situation is too bleak for Him.

When healing angels come, don't be surprised if you feel overcome by the Spirit and begin to faint under His supernatural power. That's okay. Angels are there ministering to you. Even right now as you're reading this, I believe God has His healing angels surrounding your life. In this chapter, I will share some testimonies and give you some instruction that will enable you to flow with them.

A Healing Angel in India

My late friend, Pastor Victor Gnanaraj, from Trichy, India, sent me a letter telling of the great supernatural encounters he had been having:

> ...my prayer closet was filled with the presence of the Lord, and the Holy Spirit spoke to me expressly that four angels are recruited for me: one of them being the angel of healing, whose name is Raphael. He brings the healing virtues from the cross of Calvary and deposits healing in sick people under my prayer requests to the Father. Ever since, miracles have happened, including fourth-stage cancer healed, kidney and gallbladder stones disappearing, etc.

Who is Raphael? There are four angels specifically mentioned by name within our Scriptures: Michael, meaning "warrior of God"; Gabriel, meaning "hero of God"; the fallen angel, Lucifer, who received a new name, Satan, meaning "adversary"; and Abaddon or Apollyon, meaning "the one who guards the bottomless pit." Within some of the Apocryphal texts, there appears another prominent angel named Raphael.[11] This name means "healing one of God," as it is a combination of *rapha*, which means "healer," and *El*, meaning God.

I think it's important to note that in the cases of both Michael and Gabriel, we gain the insight that it was not the angel who performed miraculous feats on his own; rather, each angel was simply a heavenly messenger for the miraculous to be delivered. It is the same with Raphael and all of His angels.

The root meaning of Raphael appears in the modern Hebrew word *rophe*, meaning "doctor of medicine," again confirming the healing function traditionally attributed to this angel. Some ancient Jewish texts say that Raphael was the angel who taught Noah about medicines and cures from evil spirits.[12] It is believed by many (and I include myself in this number) that Raphael was the angel in John 5:1–4 who stirred the miracle waters in the pool of Bethesda. The exact name of the angel, however, is not as important as knowing his purpose. From the Scriptures, we can glean insight to know with certainty that God has angels of healing available to minister to and for His children.

11. Tobit 3:16–17.
12. Jubilees 10:12, also part of the Apocrypha.

An Angel Delivers Gifts of Healing

On May 7, 1946, the famous evangelist William Branham had a life-changing encounter with a healing angel who imparted special supernatural gifts to him. These gifts would be used to carry God's healing power to people wherever Branham traveled. The angel told Branham, "God has sent you to take a gift of healing to the peoples of the world. If you will be sincere and can get the people to believe you, nothing shall stand before your prayer, not even cancer."[13]

Although Branham's encounter was very unusual, and his prophetic gift and ability to discern specific illnesses has not been duplicated in recent years, people all over the world have reported encounters with God's healing angels. In fact, it seems to me that more angel encounters are happening now than ever before in all of history. That makes sense because the pages of the final book of the Bible, the last-days book of Revelation, is filled with the greatest number of angel encounters. The closer we get to the end of time, the more we should expect an increase of angelic activity.

JESUS CHRIST IS THE GREAT PHYSICIAN, BUT HIS ANGELS ARE THE NURSE PRACTITIONERS.

Branham was a forerunner, but we have the privilege of continuing to run the race set before us. As our eyes are focused on Jesus, He will surround us with His ministering spirits everywhere we go. Jesus Christ is the Great Physician, but His angels are the nurse practitioners.

Angels in a Hospital Room

A few years ago, our daughter, Liberty, was struck with a sudden severe illness that required her to be placed on life support in the hospital. I have come to call this our "Psalm 23 experience," for I actually felt as

13. Gordon Lindsay, *William Branham: A Man Sent from God* (self-published), 77.

though we were walking through the valley of the shadow of death. God was with us throughout this entire ordeal, and we know that because we believe His Word, but one night, while Janet was taking the night shift so that I could get some sleep, something supernatural happened in Liberty's hospital room. Janet explains it this way:

> That night, the lights were turned off, except for a little glow that came through the pulled curtain that gave Liberty some privacy. The nurses would come in and out to check Liberty's stats and levels as she lay there peacefully, completely sedated and on life support. Joshua and I, among other family and friends, had created an atmosphere of peace and faith in Liberty's room. We did this by playing SpiritSpa[14] instrumental worship, declaring God's healing Word, and speaking words of life over her.
>
> At around 2 a.m., I was praying in a chair beside Liberty's bed when I began to feel an overwhelming sense of peace and could suddenly sense that I was not alone. Of course, the hospital staff was nearby, but that wasn't the company I was discerning. I sensed that healing angels were there. I began to feel a cool wind in the room and was in awe of the thick presence of God's glory. This brought me great encouragement and elevated my faith even further for the manifestation of Liberty's total miracle. I received strength in that moment to continue standing firm on the promises of God.
>
> The amazing thing is that when I was experiencing this, some nurses pulled the curtain back to enter the room and stopped abruptly. They could also feel an immediate climate change on our side of the curtain. They went back and forth and kept commenting on what they were feeling. They even said that they could feel a special "peace" in Liberty's room.
>
> There are healing angels that bring the gift of peace and strength, and that night I could tangibly feel their presence. Of course, this opened up an opportunity for me to share once again

14. Joshua Mills, *SpiritSpa*, available as a digital download or CD at https://shop. newwineinternational.org.

with the nurses that God was with us. His angels were surrounding Liberty's life.

Seventeen days after she went into the hospital, Liberty returned home with a clean bill of health. This was contrary to all of the negative reports and diagnoses we had received on that first day—and the following days. Our God heals. His name is *Jehovah Rapha*, the Lord, our Healer. Sometimes, He will send healing angels into the midst of difficult situations to deliver peace and strength to those who are in the process of waiting for a healing manifestation.

Personally, I don't understand why some healings take place quickly while others seem to be more gradual. But I'm thankful for healing in any form that God wants to release it. Aren't you? Why don't you welcome His healing angels to come now and minister His purposes in His own way in your life?

Healing Angels in Indonesia

Quite a few years ago, while we were ministering in Jakarta, Indonesia, our hosts invited us to visit their home so that we could pray with some of their family members. We must have been praising the Lord quite loudly because one of their next-door neighbors stopped by to see what was happening. We quickly learned that this man had been suffering with severe pain in his right arm and joints. Janet and I told him that God wanted to heal him, and we began to minister to him by laying our hands on his arm. We had confidence that as we stretched out our hands, God would extend His healing arm as well as His healing angels to surround this man who was in desperate need of restoration. At the time, we were unaware that the man was not yet saved, but I believe God always finds a way to set up these divine appointments!

After a short prayer, the man told us that his arm felt much better, and then, he hurriedly left. Several minutes later, however, he returned, wanting to know why his arm was covered with a shiny golden substance. It was obvious to us that ministering angels had been at work, delivering both healing and miracles! The man's newly-healed arm was completely covered in a shimmering golden glory, and he was shocked by it.[15] This golden glory on his arm was a sign that made him wonder, and this gave us the opportunity to share more about the goodness of God. Through this encounter, the man received Jesus Christ into his heart as personal Lord and Savior. As we continued ministering throughout Indonesia, many miracles happened everywhere we went, and it was evident that God's angels were both going ahead of us and following behind us.

Sometimes healing angels appear in full form, while at other times, we only see a glimpse or partial vision of their activity. The most important thing is to be aware of their presence, so that we can cooperate more fully with what they are doing and focus on bringing glory to Jesus.

Learning to Co-Labor with Angels

As I minister around the world, it is common for healing angels to appear in our meetings, with the visible results of physical bodies being healed and miracles reported wherever we go. When we speak God's Word with power, angels show up and begin working, according to the scriptural assignment that they've been given. I've discovered that all healing ministries have healing angels available to work with them—because it's the Word of God that releases those angels. Unfortunately, not every minister is aware of these God-sent helpers, which can hinder the flow.

God provides healing angels to stand behind his ministers as they pray for the sick. These angels are stationed there, positioned as support workers for God's anointed servants. When healing angels arrive, they bring a tangible atmosphere of healing with them. At times, they may deliver the specific and necessary miracle that is needed in that moment, and it becomes our responsibility to receive it by faith and impart it to those who desperately need a touch from God. At other times, they wait for our faith to boldly extract the sickness and disease from those who are suffering. They are waiting for us to hand these spirits of infirmity to them so they can carry them away. These are just some of the ways we can co-labor with the healing angels.

15. If you've never heard of this supernatural sign before, I would encourage you to read my book, *Moving in Glory Realms*, where it is explained more fully. It will bring scriptural understanding and get you activated in deeper realms of God's manifest presence, with visible signs and wonders.

Releasing Healing Angels Through Prayer

In the book of Daniel, an angel appeared to the prophet in a vision, saying, *"Don't be afraid, Daniel. Since the first day you began to pray for understanding and to humble yourself before your God, your request has been heard in heaven. I have come in answer to your prayer"* (Daniel 10:12 NLT).

It's vital for you to realize how important your prayers are to God. When you pray, God sends His angels in response to the words you speak. This is exactly what happened in the above verse. The angel Gabriel told Daniel that he had been sent to him on behalf of the prayers the prophet had offered to the Lord. Your prayers of healing have the ability to touch heaven, and dispatch healing angels to earth on divine assignments. We can find abundant scriptural precedent for this throughout the Bible. Consider these instances for example:

+ When Abraham interceded in prayer, two angels were released to go to Sodom in order to save Lot and his family. (Genesis 18:22–33; 19:1–25)

+ Moses prayed and an angel stood between the army of Egypt and the children of Israel, bringing great deliverance for God's chosen people. (Exodus 14:15–20)

+ King Hezekiah prayed to the Lord for help, and God responded by sending His angel to kill 185,000 enemy soldiers. (2 Kings 19:15–19, 35–37)

+ After Jesus prayed on the Mount of Olives, an angel from heaven appeared and strengthened Him during His time of need. (Luke 22:41–43)

+ When Cornelius prayed, an angel was sent to his home, bringing a divine connection to Spirit-birthed revelation that resulted in the salvation of his household. (Acts 10)

+ Believers prayed for Peter's release from prison and God responded by sending an angel to bring supernatural deliverance. (Acts 12:5–11)

In each of these instances, prayers were offered to God, not to angels. But the result was that God chose to loose His angels in response to these prayers. This is one of the ways in which God accomplishes His purposes in the earth. When we pray for healing, we should expect healing angels to show up, bringing God's miracles with them.

New Wine Angels

Several years ago, a group of healing angels showed up during one of my meetings at Winter Campmeeting, in Ashland, Virginia. I didn't see them at first, but Sister Jane Lowder, the camp director, saw in a vision that they were present. When she shared what she was seeing, I could certainly feel their presence in the room. She went on to describe their unusual appearance. They were wearing hospital scrubs, looking like doctors or nurses. This was one of the ways we knew that these were healing angels. God was giving Sister Jane a visual understanding of their purpose for coming into the meeting.

Each of these healing angels came into the room carrying what appeared to be an intravenous drip. God made it known to us, through a prophetic word, that instead of there being natural medicine inside their bags, these IVs were filled with supernatural "new wine." Matthew explains "new wine" as a fresh movement of God that cannot be seen through eyes that only recognize the old ways of doing things: *"Neither do people pour new wine into old wineskins. If they do, the skins will burst; the wine will run out and the wineskins will be ruined. No, they pour new wine into new wineskins, and both are preserved"* (Matthew 9:17 NIV). In this case, the new wine was the life of the Spirit and heavenly healing for those who were thirsty for it.

I understood that these angels were being assigned to various individuals present in the meeting, those who had been standing in faith for a long time and felt as though they couldn't stand much longer. God was giving them a heavenly jump-start, an angelic infusion of new wine for strength, restoration, and healing. In that meeting, there was no struggle or striving for miracles. Those angels had been sent to bring the flow of God's goodness into the lives of those who desperately needed it.

I have become aware of these same angels several times since that initial encounter, and whenever I see them, I mention it to those who are present. These new-wine angels come to minister a direct infusion of healing.

Welcome God's healing angels into your life and learn how to cultivate an atmosphere for miracles to occur with ease.

Special Deliveries from Heaven

Because angels are *"ministering spirits"* sent to serve the heirs of salvation, they love to bring us special deliveries from heaven. Many people who have been caught up to behold the glories of heaven have reported seeing a large warehouse containing what seems to be unlimited spare body parts needed by people in the earth. We understand that our prayers and declarations of healing cause creative miracles to come forth. In the Spirit realm, we are simply moving those much-needed body parts from heaven to earth, and one of the ways God allows those creative miracles to come is through the ministry service of His healing angels.

Once, while I was ministering at the Healing Rooms in Spokane, Washington, I saw in a vision what appeared to be a lifejacket being carried by an angel. In my spirit, I understood that this represented a new pair of lungs being delivered through the ministry of a healing angel. (Our lungs really do serve a life-saving function.) I declared what I was seeing and, sure enough, a lady approached me after the meeting and told me that those lungs had been for her. She said that as I was declaring the miracle, she could breathe deeper and more fully than ever before. In the past, she always felt winded and had trouble walking any distance without becoming short of breath, but that night, she received her miracle, and her breathing changed. She believed that she had received those new lungs!

In the Spirit, I saw many other healings that night, and as I declared them by faith, I knew that healing angels were being dispatched to minister to those who needed a touch of God in their physical bodies.

Healing Angels with Backpacks

My friend Joan Hunter has a great healing ministry. She has operated in this gift for many years, but only recently she discovered that God had assigned healing angels not only to her ministry as a whole, but also to the individual services where she ministers. As she was preaching in one meeting, she saw angels hovering over the people in attendance. She wrote:

These angels didn't have wings; they had an arm span. They were gliding, like flying, over the congregation, and each of them had a big hump on his back. I couldn't figure it out; I couldn't make out what that hump was.[16]

So often in the spiritual realm, we see things that don't make sense to us in the natural. When this happens, we must remain at peace and continue pressing forward, trusting that the answers will come as God sees fit. Don't become distressed if something doesn't make sense to you at first. As long as you have the peace of God, you can rest in Him.

IF YOU WANT TO MOVE IN GREATER HEALING MINISTRY, YOU MUST LEARN HOW TO MOVE WITH THE HEALING ANGELS WHO HAVE BEEN ASSIGNED TO WORK WITH YOU.

Joan began to call out words of knowledge for healing and creative miracles, particularly a new heart. She continued the story:

Instantly I saw this angel reach backward into the hump, and at that moment the person I was praying for moved abruptly as if he had been hit by something. In that moment, he received a brand-new heart.[17]

Joan continued to describe those humps on the backs of the angels as if they were backpacks filled with body parts needed for that particular service.

---

16. Joan Hunter, "Healing Angels Deliver New Body Parts," *Angel Stories*, Jonathan Nixon, compiler (Lake Mary, FL: Charisma House, 2014), 13.
17. Ibid.

Some people have seen angels bringing gifts into meetings in various sized boxes, filled with body parts, healing oil, or other blessings. I have seen these healing angels come in many different ways. The method or appearance isn't what matters; the ministry fruit that remains is what is important to us. When you learn how to work with these angels (and we will get to that in later chapters), the results will be phenomenal. Although some people may try to dismiss your awareness of these angels, it will become impossible for them to dismiss the results! If you want to move in greater healing ministry, you must learn how to move with the healing angels who have been assigned to work with you.

Healing Angels Assist in Supernatural Surgery

When I was a teenager, my pastor's wife had a heavenly experience at the altar of our church one Sunday. The Lord and His angels began performing supernatural surgery on her heart. She had suffered from a weak heart for the majority of her life, but as she was caught up in the glory realms, it was as though she was lying on heaven's operating table, as God and His angels performed open-heart surgery on her. During this supernatural encounter, God physically replaced her damaged heart with a brand new one!

After this happened, she returned to her doctor for a check-up and received the exciting report: without natural explanation, her heart was now like that of a sixteen-year-old. God had physically healed her, and it was glorious!

Healing angels can minister to much more than a physical ailment or pain. The Scriptures promise:

He heals the broken in heart, and binds up their wounds.

(Psalm 147:3)

Your heart is important to God, and He places a high value on it. (See Proverbs 4:23.) Personally, I believe that He does some of His heart-healing through the ministry service of angels.

We know that there are many angels who surround God and work in His presence, and just being in that atmosphere changes everything. In our meetings around the world, we often hear testimonies from people reporting that God has healed their hearts emotionally. Sometimes people have carried deep guilt, shame, regret, or rejection in their hearts for many years, and God wants to heal your heart from that too! I believe He has commissioned angels over your life to help you heal from past wounds and to encourage your heart to be open for all the love He desires to bring into your life today and tomorrow.

If you're ready to start *Seeing Angels*, let's pray:

Father, in the name of Jesus, I know that You are the Great Physician and that all healing comes from You. I stand in agreement with Your Word for complete and total healing to manifest in my spirit, mind, and body. I command every spirit of sickness and infirmity to leave, as You send Your angels of healing to surround my life and minister Your healing touch to me. I choose to step into the miracle waters of Your Spirit and life. In the mighty name of Jesus, amen!

4

Angels of Abundant Provision

The blessing of the LORD, it makes rich,
and He adds no sorrow with it.
Proverbs 10:22

I have several angels of provision who travel with me and watch over the financial affairs of our family and our ministry. One of those angels is named Prosperity. Prosperity stands about nine feet tall. He is very joyful. I've never heard him speak a word, but I've often heard him laugh, and when he does, it's always one of those deep, infectious belly laughs.

Prosperity's laugh makes me laugh too, for somehow, that manifestation of joy is connected with the supernatural manifestation of provision he brings. His laughter seems to change the atmosphere. The reason for this, I have discovered, is that Prosperity carries the atmosphere of heaven's abundance with him, so that everywhere he goes, there is a shimmering sparkle and glow in the air around him. Sometimes we even get to see these spiritual sparkles begin to manifest around us in the natural as a golden glory.

Something else unique about Prosperity is this: although his skin seems to be like porcelain, he has golden hair, golden coins are continually pouring off of his luminescent robe, and he is dripping with what appears to be liquid gold. This is the visible manifestation of the gift Prosperity has been sent to deliver. He literally leaves a trail of blessing behind him everywhere he goes.

I've never seen Prosperity fly, and I don't think he has any wings. At least I've never seen them, but I suppose it's possible for him to move in any way the Lord needs him to. Another thing I should mention is that although Prosperity is covered in beautiful gold (representing the glory and riches of God) and seems to disperse his riches freely, he is very humble. He never brings any glory to himself. Instead, he serves the purposes of God to bring all glory to Jesus Christ.

I have seen this deep humility on the few occasions when I've had the privilege of looking into Prosperity's fascinating hazel eyes. All I could see was the glory of God. The true blessing of God always points you not to the blessing itself, but to the One who blesses. God's angels are carriers who deliver God's blessings, but they are never the one from whom those blessings originate. That's why we must learn to always point our hearts and eyes toward Jesus.

Unusual Types of Provision

There are many different types of angels of provision that we can discover within the sacred Scriptures, although they may not be apparent at first glance. God has many angels of prosperity, angels of blessing, angels of financial replenishment, and angels of abundant wealth and overflow, and each time they appear in the lives of God's people, they bring with them an array of extraordinary forms of provision. This would include the "angel food," the manna that God rained down on the Israelites as they traveled through the wilderness. (See Psalm 78:23–25.)

Once, while I was ministering along with several other speakers at a conference at Valley Harvest Church in Neenah, Wisconsin, many supernatural signs of provision began appearing in the meetings. Several people received dramatic, creative-miracle healings in their bodies, while others reported gemstones, including diamonds, raining down on them as they were worshiping the Lord. One night, just before I took the platform to speak, two ladies found manna visibly materializing for them on their front-row seats. Although the spiritual bodies of angels were unseen that night, it was apparent that they were present in the meeting, bringing gifts to us from heaven. This heavenly manna seemed to be just like the bread of angels spoken about in the Scriptures, *"It was white like coriander seed and tasted like wafers made with honey"* (Exodus 16:31 NIV). I have heard testimonies from many people around the world who have received this supernatural gift, and I think it's unusual but absolutely wonderful!

That evening, several people took the manna as their bread for communion, along with water that had supernaturally been turned into a heavenly wine. What an experience we had in the glory of the Lord! These are the things that happen when angels of provision make their presence known!

Angels of Blessing

When God first began reintroducing me to the angelic realm, I picked up a copy of the book *Angels on Assignment* by Roland Buck, a book that challenged my faith to believe God for greater interaction with the angels that surrounded my life on a daily basis. Pastor Buck shared many testimonies about his divine visitations with the angel Gabriel (yes, the same angel that appeared to Mary and others in the Bible). In one chapter, he spoke about receiving an unusual provision from heaven:

> During a visit one night, Gabriel said that God had sent me a little gift for my strength and energy as he handed me a round wafer approximately five inches in diameter and 5/8 inch thick that looked like bread. He instructed me to eat it; so I did. It had the taste of honey. When I finished the bread, he gave me a silver-like ladle filled with what appeared to be water. I drank every drop of it, and an overwhelming desire to praise and worship God instantly came over me. Rivers of praise billowed up to God, bubbling up out of my innermost being, and for days after I drank this liquid, there was a sensation of "fizzing" inside of my veins. What an indescribably pleasant and exhilarating feeling it was! The effects were astounding because the first day after I ate the wafer and drank the water, I lost five pounds! The second day, I lost another five pounds! The third and fourth days, another five pounds each day! Then it tapered off to about a pound a day. I had an excess of "flab," and that is all gone now.[18]

---

18. Buck, *Angels on Assignment*, 42.

In a previous chapter, I mentioned the angels of protection that shut the lions' mouths and saved Daniel's life. But do you realize that there were also angels of blessing involved who provided food for Daniel while he was in that lions' den? The apocryphal fourteenth chapter of Daniel tells that when Daniel was trapped in the lions' den, an angel appeared to the prophet Habakkuk and instructed him to carry dinner to Daniel so that he would have something to eat during his time of trial. The angel then proceeded to lift Habakkuk through the air by his hair and held him suspended over the lions' den so that he could deliver that meal. It seems that even though the mouths of the lions were shut, Daniel was hungry.[19]

If that ancient story is true, God assigned an angel that picked up Habakkuk and brought him into the lions' den so that he could deliver the food he had prepared for Daniel. That's how much God cares for you and me!

The Bible makes it clear that our father Abraham was accustomed to having angels of blessing lead him as he traveled in the land of Canaan. (See Genesis 18:2, 22:11, 24:40.) You and I can have the same blessing as Abraham.[20] In other words, angels of blessing can come into our lives and lead us to the right place at the right time and to the right people. Praise God!

Angles That Release Miracle Money

In our meetings, it is common for people to receive money miracles as they enjoy the presence of God. One afternoon, while I was ministering in Budapest, Hungary, people testified about money supernaturally appearing in their pockets, purses, and wallets, along with many other financial breakthroughs. Angels are constantly moving, activated by people's generous giving and by speaking God's Word over their finances.

God's angels are not hindered by harsh economic conditions or monetary recessions. They are released to change the financial atmosphere around you, and I've seen this happen all over the world.

While I was ministering in Auckland, New Zealand, the Spirit spoke to me about supernatural bank account deposits being made. I saw angels

---

19. Daniel 14:33–39 is considered to be scriptural canon by Orthodox Christians.
20. See Galatians 3:14.

going forth and putting money into people's bank accounts. I spoke it out loud, declaring what I had seen, and an unusual generosity broke out in the building. It wasn't until the next day that we heard the testimony of two different ladies who had received those supernatural bank account deposits. Overnight, one lady received thirty-eight thousand dollars and another lady received forty-one thousand dollars in their bank accounts. This was unexpected and unexplainable in the natural, but God allowed it to happen through the ministry of His angels.

I shared this testimony later when ministering in Phoenix, Arizona, and a woman reported receiving more than twenty thousand dollars into her bank account, again unexplainable by natural reasons. While I was ministering in San Jose, California, a woman named Vera went back to her hotel room after the meeting and was surprised to witness an angel shooting like a flash of lightening across her room. She reported:

> Suddenly a light zoomed past my peripheral vision and landed in my hotel room. It happened faster than I can even describe. I went over to the bed, where I saw the angel land, and I began spouting off every prophetic promise and declaration I could think of from the past seven years...until I eventually erupted into laughter.
>
> During the meeting, Joshua had said that God was restoring things from the past seven years and that we needed to be in remembrance of God's promises and prophecies over our lives. The encounter ended, but a season of acceleration began! I ended up making more money in the following three days than I had made in my business in an entire year! It all happened so fast!

God can use His angels to change your financial condition overnight, as you are faithful to do what you are called to do. After ministering in East London, South Africa, I received this beautiful testimony from a pastor there:

> Since you've come to minister to us, we've seen an explosion in our ministry, especially in the area of money appearing in people's pockets, wallets, etc. Most of our students are from poor African nations such as Zimbabwe, and they've now been on fire for God

since you preached at our conference. They recently went on a mission trip to Mozambique, and God supernaturally provided in excess of six thousand dollars for the trip. They live lives of radical generosity and have even trusted God for the finances to buy our church an expensive sound system (which God has supernaturally provided for)! We love seeing these young students madly in love with Jesus Christ, laying down their lives and trusting God for the impossible!

It doesn't matter who you are or where you live. Your current financial situation is not an obstacle for God. It's just another miracle waiting to happen.

The Bible speaks of a time when Peter was asked by local tax collectors whether or not Jesus paid His taxes. Peter answered, yes, and then, when he went to speak to Jesus about the matter, Jesus gave him the simple instruction to go fishing: "*We don't want to offend them, so go down to the lake and throw in a line. Open the mouth of the first fish you catch, and you will find a large silver coin. Take it and pay the tax for both of us*" (Matthew 17:27 NLT). We don't know for sure how this all came about, but I think it's quite possible that angels were involved in putting that coin in the fish's mouth. I am convinced that angels are involved in a lot more of the situations of our lives than we ever realize.

Angels of Replenishment

God has angels that release miracle money for believers, and He also has angels that minister the supernatural replenishment of provisions.

My friend, the late evangelist Edgar Baillie, was well-known for the bottle of anointing oil he carried everywhere he went. It was supernatural. I say this because one day, the oil began to appear out of nowhere. No matter how much of that oil he used to anoint the masses, it never ran out. Doesn't that sound like the story in 1 Kings 17, when the prophet Elijah asked a widow to use her limited supply of flour and oil to bake him a cake? The Scriptures tell us that although she used everything she had, "*no matter how much they used, there was always plenty left in the containers, just as the LORD had promised through Elijah!*" (1 Kings 17:16 TLB).

Although angels are not specifically mentioned in this passage (because that was not the focus of the story), I personally believe that angels of replenishment were involved in this miracle of divine supply. Angels can bend physical laws to minister supernatural overflow to those who are willing to receive it.

Some time ago, Edgar shared an unusual angelic encounter that happened to him while he was living in California. At that time, he and his family were so broke, they had nothing in their cupboards to eat. While Edgar and his wife were at a nearby Kathryn Kuhlman meeting, his son Bruce heard a commotion in the kitchen as he sat in the living room. It sounded as though other people had somehow entered the house, even though he was certain that the back door was firmly closed and locked. Though startled, Bruce also felt the overwhelming presence of the Lord. This strong presence made it virtually impossible for him to move from the chair in which he was sitting. As he sat there pondering what was happening, he heard cupboard doors being opened and then slammed shut again.

When Edgar and his wife arrived home, he said, "It sounds like somebody's in the kitchen."

Bruce answered, "Yes, they've been in there for a while now."

When Edgar went to see who was in their kitchen, he was surprised to discover no one there at all. He opened the refrigerator door and found that it was stocked full of food. He checked the cupboards, and they were also full of canned goods. Edgar later told me, "There was bacon and eggs.... God knows exactly what I like!"[21]

This miracle testimony thrilled me! I love to hear and share testimonies about God's abundant provision in our lives. But what really intrigues me about this particular testimony is the activation that caused the miracle to take place. Edgar continued:

Now, let me tell you what caused this. That particular day, we had gone to a Kathryn Kuhlman meeting in Los Angeles, and when the collection bucket came, I put everything I had left into the offering.

---

21. Edgar Baillie speaking at the New Wine International Signs and Wonders Summer Campmeeting, in London, Ontario, Canada; July 2003.

There it is! Everything we do in obedience to God becomes a seed for a future harvest. Something the Spirit has taught us is that we must make the connection between the natural and the supernatural worlds. God will ask us to do something *possible* so that He can do something *impossible*. Edgar gave a sacrificial offering that day, not knowing what the exact outcome would be, but he did know the truth of Philippians 4:19: *"my God shall supply."*

EVERYTHING WE DO IN OBEDIENCE TO GOD
BECOMES A SEED FOR A FUTURE HARVEST.
GOD WILL ASK US TO DO SOMETHING *POSSIBLE*
SO THAT HE CAN DO SOMETHING *IMPOSSIBLE*.

In Acts, we find the story of a Roman centurion who was also *"devout and God-fearing; he gave generously to those in need and prayed to God regularly"* (Acts 10:2 NIV). At 3 o'clock in the afternoon, an angel visited him and instructed him to send servants to the apostle Peter, who, simultaneously, was having visions of eating non-kosher foods. Angels used this generous, non-Jewish centurion to expand God's generosity of faith to the Gentiles.

There is a direct connection between our generous giving on earth and the activation of our angels that bring supernatural provision from heaven. The angel who appeared to Cornelius in his home at three o'clock in the afternoon told him that he had come in direct response to his generous giving, and angels respond to our giving too!

How I Met Prosperity

I already told you about my angel of provision named Prosperity. What I didn't mention was that I initially met him in a dream. We had just returned home from a ministry trip to Singapore and had a few hours turnaround time before we needed to head back out on the road again. While Janet did our laundry, I decided to lie down and rest for a while before having to board another airplane. I fell into a deep sleep and was quickly taken into a dream.

In my dream, I saw the angel Prosperity coming toward me. I had never seen him before. This was to be the first of many visitations I have had from him over the years. As I said before, his appearance was dazzling. He was absolutely covered with gold and radiated the glory of God.

Janet came running into the room, not realizing that I had fallen asleep and was having this wonderful dream. She said to me, "Joshua, I washed all the clothes and put them in the dryer, but just now, as I was taking them out of the dryer, they were covered with gold!" God was taking us into something deeper, and I got very elated about it.

It came to me that one of the first and most important things we must do when God is bringing us into an encounter like this is not to hold back. Give yourself wholly to the encounter. Engage with the heavenly realm. One of the greatest ways you can do that, especially when there is a prosperity encounter involved, is by generously sowing a financial gift in faith.

Earlier in the afternoon, as we were driving home from the airport, a minister friend of mine had called me. She told me that her air conditioner had broken and she needed $3,600 to replace it. She hadn't called to ask me for money, but rather to ask for prayer. I prayed with her over the phone and felt the presence of God fill our conversation. I had full confidence that God would meet her need. In the rush of activities, I had forgotten about that matter, rushed home, gone to sleep, and experienced my dream. But when Janet said that golden glory was manifesting all over our clothes, I knew what I needed to do. I said, "Janet, we need to sow that $3,600. We'll have to clean out our savings account to do it, but we need to sow that money into our minister friend so that we can fully engage with this prosperity encounter."

Janet agreed.

I picked up the phone and called the minister back. She was in a different time zone, three hours ahead of us, and I woke her up. I apologized and then said, "I needed to call you because we're having an encounter with an angel of prosperity, and we've decided to take our savings and sow them into your need. We want to pay that $3,600 to purchase a brand-new air conditioner for you."

The lady immediately began to weep. God had provided for her need. How had He done it? According to His riches in glory, He had sent an angel to me, that I would be blessed and become a blessing to her. Could I have possibly suffered loss in that situation? Never! I may have cleaned out my savings account, but God was not about to let me remain in lack. He was ready to bring increase to my life.

I began to change clothes before leaving to catch our next flight. When I put on my shorts, I put my hand into the pockets and felt what seemed like money in there. I was sure I had not left any money in those shorts, but now there was a twenty-dollar bill. Twenty dollars is not a lot these days, but that's not the point. This was a supernatural sign from God that because I had just sowed, He would supply my needs.

What can twenty dollars do for you? Not much. Even if it had been forty, sixty, or eighty dollars, that still doesn't go very far in North America. But when we can be thankful for the little, God can turn it into much. God takes pleasure in the prosperity of His people.

Lord, we thank You for Your signs.

The Bible says that signs will come to confirm God's Word. I took the unexplained appearance of that twenty-dollar bill as a sign that God's Word was true in my life, and I was filled with joy.

When our son Lincoln, who was very young at the time, went to put on his shorts, he had money in his pockets too, and he got excited. Soon the whole family was rejoicing and thanking God. Even though it was not a huge harvest, we were thankful that God was bringing something new into our lives through this encounter with the angel of prosperity. Later, when we began to relay this testimony by phone to our office manager in Canada, she explained that at that very same time, she had begun receiving a shimmering appearance of golden glory on her forearms and all over her pants as well. This had become a corporate encounter for us all!

Soon after we got to our next ministry engagement, I set up my computer and checked for any emails so I could take care of some ministry business. The first email in my inbox was from Singapore. It said, "After you left, offerings for your ministry continued to come in."

Wow! This was not something that happened very often. Once we leave a place, it is very rare to have the people there keep giving to us. There are so many demands on people's incomes and so many other causes to give to. I am always thankful for whatever generosity is displayed to us, but I never expect it to continue. The believers in Singapore now sent us another offering, nearly equal to the first offering they had given us—and more than the amount we had just sowed for the air conditioner. Angels were at work in our lives because God takes pleasure in our prosperity.

We were feeling very blessed by all of this and started sowing more into the glory. God was giving us more than we needed so we could invest in His work as He led us by His Spirit.

An Angel Brings Us Our First Home

For the first eleven years of our marriage, we would write the words "a new home" on the back of our offering envelopes. For eleven years, we sowed this way, believing for a new home. We were faithful with our tithes and our offerings, but we were also faithful to sow seed for this special miracle.

After eleven years of doing this, our landlord in California contacted us early one day from Seattle, where he was living. Janet and I were still in bed, checking our emails. He said, "We're ready to retire and come back to live in our home, so you and Janet will have to move within the next few months."

After receiving this news, I looked at Janet and said, "I'm tired of moving from place to place." We had gone from apartment to apartment, and rental house to rental house. We lived in basement apartments, we lived in one-room apartments, and we lived in two-room condos. Housing is very expensive in California, so we had lived in some homes that were nice (when we were able to get a good deal) and others that were not so nice (when it seemed like no good deal was available). I was tired of moving.

I said, "We have sown our seed now for eleven years, believing for a new home. We have an angel of prosperity working in our life. I just know that God is going to do this miracle for us. We will move one more time, and it will be into our own home."

Janet looked back at me and agreed, "Yes, we will move one more time, and it will be into our own home." We sat there in bed, holding each other's hands, and prayed together, thanking God that He would make a way for us to move into a new home. Then, we got up, got dressed, and went to our ministry office.

After a while, there was a knock at the door. When I opened it, there stood Ingrid, the landlady of our ministry office.

Ingrid didn't waste any time. She said, "Do you need a home?"

I said, "As a matter of fact, I do."

Ingrid had no way of knowing that our other landlord had called that very morning to let us know that we would soon have to move out. She said, "I think I know the perfect home for you."

I said, "Okay." And we arranged to go with her the following Tuesday to see the home she had in mind. It was for sale.

On Tuesday, Janet and I walked through the home and agreed that it would be the perfect home for us. There was only one problem: We had no money to buy. And if you have no money to buy, no matter how perfect the house is for you, and no matter how perfect the timing of the purchase is, it won't do you any good. People selling homes want to see the money. That's just how it is.

We agreed with Ingrid that the house was perfect for us. Then she asked the all-important question: "Do you have money to buy the home?"

I said, "We don't."

She didn't seem to be overly troubled by this revelation. She said, "Well, why don't you go talk to the bank. They're giving some home loans to various people right now, trying to get these older homes sold. It can't hurt to go talk to them." So we made an appointment to speak with a broker at the bank.

We had spoken with the broker for less than five minutes before it became apparent that we would not qualify for any of the loans this bank offered. That was a dead end.

I decided to call Ingrid. She was the one who had suggested that we contact the bank, and maybe she would have some other ideas. Sure enough, she did. She suggested that we make an appointment with a different bank, so that's what we did. But once again, we were quickly turned down. They could not give us the loan we needed.

Before long, Ingrid called us once more. "I heard you were not approved for the loan," she said.

"Yes," I answered, "although they will loan to almost anyone, they would not loan to us. We have no money and no established credit."

What Ingrid said next startled me. "I knew they were not going to give you the money."

"What?" I asked. "Then why did you send me to those banks if you knew they wouldn't give me the money?"

"Because," she said, "I wanted to see if you were serious or not."

What was this all about? I was wondering.

Ingrid continued, "It doesn't matter that the banks won't give you the money. I have lots of money, and I'll give you all the money you need." And she did. We were able to buy the house and have enjoyed it ever since. It is a miracle house, and I believe it came to us through the ministry of my angel Prosperity.

WHEN YOU GET YOUR EYES FOCUSED ON JESUS, YOU DON'T HAVE TO LOOK FOR MONEY; MONEY WILL GET UP AND COME LOOKING FOR YOU.

I don't know how it all transpired exactly, but in time, I decided that the angel may have gone to Ingrid's house early that first morning and whispered something in her ear, got her out of bed, and told her to go to our office and knock on my door. I didn't go looking for money; *God sent Ingrid to us.* When you get your eyes focused on Jesus, you don't have to look for money; money will get up and come looking for you. There is money coming to you on the wings of angels.

Ingrid not only offered to hold the mortgage on the house; she said she would do it at a lower interest rate than the banks were charging. "Also," she said, "you can pay it off as quickly or as slowly as you want or need to."

Wow! What bank does that?

We soon signed the papers, and the house became ours. It was the favor of God that brought it all about.

An Angel Leads Me to Be Debt Free

Not too long after we had moved into our new home, I went to minister at a small church in New England. As I made my way toward the baggage claim area, I could hear the voice of the host pastor. He was laughing, but we couldn't yet see each other. As I turned a corner, we came face to face. He said, "I knew you were coming."

"How did you know?" I asked.

He said, "Because a big angel came out ahead of you. He looked really jolly, and he was covered in gold. There was golden glory and also gold coins all spilling out from him. I knew you were right behind him."

The amazing thing is: I hadn't seen Prosperity walking ahead of me, but God allowed my host to see him very clearly! I hadn't told him anything about this angel, but he described him to me exactly as I had seen him. The Lord reminded me of the Scripture that says: *"Behold, I send an angel before you, to keep you in the way, and to bring you into the place which I have prepared"* (Exodus 23:20). God assigns His angels to surround us, making sure that our endeavors are blessed, favored, successful, and directed by Him.

Although that New England congregation was small, I had a wonderful time there, ministering in the glory that weekend. God did many miracles for us. In one of the meetings, the host pastor said, "I want to do this: I want to receive just one offering. I don't want to receive a bunch of offerings. And I want that one offering to be for Joshua. I want us all to bless him, and so I'm giving you an opportunity to sow into his life." That was about all he said. He didn't go into any long teaching on giving; he just presented the opportunity in that way. But, amazingly, someone came up to me and handed me a large check that was sufficient to pay off my new home in full. One check paid it all!

Again, money came looking for me; I didn't go looking for money. When the angels of God are working in your life, that's what will happen: Money will come looking for you.

Now, don't get your eyes on money. The Bible makes it very clear:

For the love of money is a root of all kinds of evil. Some people, eager for money, have wandered from the faith and pierced themselves with many griefs. (1 Timothy 6:10 NIV)

Don't look for money and you won't have to worry about manipulating the system or getting your heart entangled with material things. *How can I get more money?* many are wondering. *How can I get rich?* You need to stop focusing on earthly treasure and start focusing on what's really important—seeking Jesus Christ over every other thing. He truly wants to be your All-in-All. "*Seek first his kingdom and his righteousness, and all these things* [everything you need] *will be given to you as well*" (Matthew 6:33 NIV).

If you're ready to start *Seeing Angels*, let's pray:

Father, I thank You for Your unlimited provision that is available to me. I thank You for the visitation of Your angels of provision in my life. Release Your angels of blessing, Your angels of prosperity, Your angels of replenishment, and Your angels of abundance, as I seek to do Your will. I thank You for meeting my every need. You are the God of more than enough. Lord, I thank You for releasing overflowing provision right now by the power of Your Spirit. In Jesus's blessed name, amen!

5

Angels of Divine Love

Then the LORD God said, "It is not good for the man to be alone.
I will make a helper who is just right for him."
Genesis 2:18 (NLT)

God desires for each and every person to find true and meaningful love in their earthly life. It was God Himself who said, *"It is not good for the man to be alone. I will make a helper who is just right for him."* God never does anything without a purpose, and I believe that for each and every one of His promises, there are angels assigned to help carry out that promise. For this reason, God has created a group of angels that I would classify as "angels of divine love," because that is their God-given assignment—helping God's children find true love. Primarily, I am speaking here of each one finding a spouse to share life with.

I was first made aware of these angels several years ago while ministering overseas, and this awareness came to me by divine revelation. There are no Scripture passages that specifically call these angels by name, and no one ever told me about these angels, but I discovered them in the Spirit and I realized that they were available for anyone who needed them!

And while they may not be mentioned by name in the Scriptures, we can certainly see angels of divine love at work in the lives of God's people over the centuries. That is, if we look for it, which is what we will do in this chapter.

FOR EACH AND EVERY ONE OF HIS PROMISES, THERE ARE ANGELS ASSIGNED TO HELP CARRY OUT THAT PROMISE.

Once I learned how to discern and activate these angels, the results were absolutely amazing! Not only do these angels of divine love help people find a lasting romantic relationship, but they also assist existing couples in maintaining a loving and passionate marriage. In other words, they help *bring* people together, and they help *keep* people together.

+ Do you desire to have an affectionate relationship, one filled with companionship, tenderness, kindness, and overflowing generosity with your soulmate?

+ Do you dream about a protective and safe marriage that allows you to share your deepest concerns and also discover the greatest peace you've ever known?

+ Do you wish that you could have perfectly clear communications with your spouse?

+ Do you want a union so fulfilling that you stay in a blissful state of satisfaction all the time?

If you answered "yes" to these questions, I have good news for you. God's angels of divine love can help you to attain all of these things. Before I share with you the keys for partnering with these divine love angels in your life, I want to first share some testimonies and explain how I discovered these angels in the first place.

Love Angels at Work in Hong Kong

Several years ago, I was preaching one Sunday morning in Hong Kong, and the Lord told me to do something I had never done before. I was instructed by the Spirit to call forth all of the single people in the church, specifically those who had a desire to marry, and minister to them. When I gave the invitation, the singles started coming. There were quite a few of them, and they filled the altar area. What was I to do next?

Fortunately, as those singles who had a desire to marry were coming forward, the Lord gave me the instructions concerning what I was to do. I was to command angels of divine love to go ahead of these young people (and some older people too) and to prosper their way so that they might find a proper spouse. In this way, I was assured, they would be brought together in a blessed union.

I did exactly what the Spirit said to me. I prayed over the young people who had gathered, and then I commanded the angels to come to their rescue. Some of those who were there could feel the Spirit in this act, and they got very excited about it. Others just stood there, not feeling much of anything. By faith, however, they received what God was promising. Then they all went back to their seats and I continued with my message.

About a year later, I went back to that same church and was thrilled when Pastor Rob Rufus told me he had never performed as many weddings before as he had done over that last year. "So many people in our congregation got married after you prayed that prayer and released those angels," he said. "It worked."

Should we be surprised that God's angels do their work? I think not. That's what they do. They work on your behalf, performing God's will for you. They work to bring His purposes forth in your life, and since His purpose is for you to have a proper mate, that's what they will work toward.

Love Angels Restore and Accelerate in Africa

Something similar happened during my visit to East London, South Africa. I gave another invitation for people who desired to be married to come forward so that I could pray with them. The Bible says, "*The man who finds a wife finds a treasure, and he receives favor from the*

LORD" (Proverbs 18:22 NLT). I believe that God wants to give you a treasure, so that you overflow in abundant favor. After we returned home, I received this thrilling testimony from Pastor Corné Pretorius:

> Well, two couples got together since then in super-fast time. The one couple (the lady turned fifty the week before the conference) was reluctant to go to the front, but she felt a prompting in her spirit. As she got to the front, she brushed past a man, and their arms briefly touched. They both felt the presence of God come strongly on them and both fell under the glory as you laid hands on them. Although they were standing on opposite sides of the room at the time, in that exact moment under the glory presence, God spoke to both of them individually about the other person— that they were "the one!" They since got engaged, and I performed the marriage a few weeks ago. The presence of God was so thick at the ceremony we could hardly even stand! Both of them came from abusive marriages, and we praise God for how He restored them and gave them this beautiful gift of marriage. What God has done in this very short period of time is truly supernatural.

Legacy and the Angels

Three days each week, our three-year-old, Legacy, goes to a home daycare where a lady named Maria does a fabulous job with all the children under her care. One day, when Janet went to pick up Legacy, Maria told her this story:

> This afternoon the children were all sitting in a little circle talking about things that have wings. I asked one child, "Do you know something that has wings?"
>
> The child said, "Yes, birds have wings."
>
> Another child said, "Butterflies have wings."
>
> Legacy raised her hand and I called on her. "What has wings, Legacy?" I asked.
>
> Legacy said, "Angels have wings."

This answer surprised me, and I said, "Well, how do you know that angels have wings?"

Legacy said, "Because I see them."

This got me very interested, and I asked her, "Where do you see them?"

Legacy said, "In my daddy's office."

When Janet told me that story, you can imagine how it touched my heart. What a blessing! This child is so pure and innocent and has a childlike faith to see in the glory realm. Then Janet told me the rest of Maria's story:

> Later that day, I decided to lead all the children in some songs, and I let them make requests. When it came Legacy's turn, I was thinking, What song might this godly child want to sing? To my surprise, Legacy said, "All the Single Ladies" (referring to a song by Beyoncé).
>
> "Legacy," I asked, "where did you hear that song?"
>
> "On the airplane," she answered.

I was thankful Legacy didn't say, "In my daddy's office." I would have been horrified! I was shocked, really shocked, when I heard that part of the story. Why had Legacy wanted to sing that particular song? That was so crazy. At the time, I just couldn't make sense of it. Then, a couple of months later, as I was relating this story one day, the Spirit spoke to me: "Legacy was prophesying!"

What? I wondered. "How could she be prophesying?"

The Spirit said, "In this day, I am releasing an increase of angels to help people find their spouses." Even Legacy knew there was a connection between angels and single ladies (and men too).

If you are single, ask the Lord to make you perceptive and receptive to His realms, so that you will understand what He is doing, how He is moving, what He is releasing, and how you are being led through it all to a proper spouse.

Angels of Divine Love for You

The LORD, the God of heaven, who brought me out of my father's household and my native land and who spoke to me and promised me on oath, saying, "To your offspring I will give this land"—he will send his angel before you so that you can get a wife for my son from there.

(Genesis 24:7 NIV)

These were the words of Abraham, spoken to his servant Eliezer, as he was giving him last-minute instructions before sending him out to find a proper bride for his son Isaac. God, he said, was also interested in this matter, so interested that He would send an angel before Eliezer to prosper his way as he sought just the right bride for the master's son. The way Abraham spoke makes me think that he was accustomed to having angels work on his behalf. They must have guided him in the past. He was absolutely sure that this angel would do the work assigned to him, and he assured Eliezer of that fact.

Imagine having the responsibility of choosing a bride for the son of a very wealthy man. That could be very dangerous, and Eliezer was wise enough to know that fact. But God had a plan to take care of the matter. He would send an angel of divine love to complete this difficult task. Eliezer was not on his own, not at all.

Now, if these Old Testament figures could be aware of the ministry of angels in their lives, how much more should we, all these years later, during this period of miraculous manifestation, expect to experience angelic help from day to day. Believe for it.

Accelerated Angelic Activity in Virginia

About a year ago, I shared some of these things with a congregation, and I invited any of the single people who desired to be married to respond to the message. Several people came forward that night. One man in particular stands out in my memory. James was believing that God would assign an angel of divine love to lead him to a new life partner. I prayed for everyone who came forward, and then all those singles, James among them, headed back to their seats.

When James got back to the seat he had been occupying, someone else was sitting there, a lady named Pam. She was late coming to the service that night because she had been held up in traffic on her way. (Do you believe in divine delays?) When Pam had arrived, the singles were in the front being prayed for, and she just took a seat that looked vacant to her.

When James got back to his seat, Pam asked him, "What were they praying for?" James explained that it had been a prayer for the single people to find a proper mate, and Pam exclaimed, "Oh my! I'm single! I should've been up there! I lost my husband about a year ago." As you can imagine, this led to James and Pam having a wonderful conversation, which led to them going on several dates, and two months later, they were married!

I was able to meet with James and Pam a few months later, and they told me their wonderful story. God has put them together, and they were spreading the gospel message everywhere they went through music and ministry. Praise God for His angels of divine love!

Please note: I would not advise anyone to jump quickly into a marriage relationship, but if you are careful to follow God's ways, you can't go wrong. His ways are always best.

The Help of an Angel in California

While I was ministering in Huntington Beach, California, I shared the story about what Legacy had seen and said. Then I asked all the single people who had a desire to marry to stand, and I proceeded to prophesy over them that angels of divine love were being assigned and released to lead them into divinely-orchestrated relationships. A lady named Roxanne was among those who stood for prayer. Later, she testified:

> While you were prophesying, it felt like somebody had put their hand on my back. I turned around, but nobody was there. I literally felt the angel or angels that were being assigned to me. I was so encouraged by that. I've had some awesome supernatural experiences in the past, but I can't recall ever feeling an angel before. I really needed that!

Roxanne hadn't been in much of a rush to get into another relationship. After experiencing heartbreak and a failed marriage, she had tried dating a few times, but somehow it just never felt quite right. She thought maybe she was just too picky and that's why she was still single. But I firmly believe that God has the right person for each of us. If we are willing to move in His divine timing and allow His angels of divine love to lead us, it will be possible to find true and lasting love in the right way.

A few months later, we received a testimony follow-up report from Roxanne:

Guess what! I met a guy. I still can't believe it. I met him just a couple weeks after that meeting where the angel placed his hand on me!

As I am writing this book, I can report that Roxanne and her "guy" are now happily married.

A Heavenly Attraction

Recently, when I had the opportunity to speak with a group in Maricopa, Arizona, about the ministry of angels, I felt compelled to share one of my own personal testimonies about these angels of divine love. Just before I started sharing, one of the ladies in the room began to smell an overwhelming scent of "musk." At first, she dismissed the aroma, but it continued to linger, and the fragrance seemed to be growing even more intense. This made her question the reason for the smell. She knew it wasn't the smell of anyone in the room because everyone was sitting down, and no one new was coming in.

In time, she began to realize that what she was smelling was a supernatural manifestation materializing in the atmosphere of the meeting. Excitedly, she began to search on her phone for an understanding of what it meant, and this is what she found: "Musk originally came from the scent glands of Asian musk deer. It contains a pheromone that brings with it an attraction for the opposite sex." She wondered if this could possibly be a sign of angels of divine love coming into the meeting that night. I think it is very possible because God's angels help bring us heavenly attraction.

The way God creates divine relationships in your life is through attraction, not through strenuous effort on your part. He connects you with people who feel drawn to you. It's all about the ease of God's glory. And that's what these angels will help you to do; they will lead you into that ease, which, in turn, will become attractive to others.

Nobody wants to be around a person who is uptight, stressed out, nit-picky, and constantly concerned with unimportant details. You are most attractive when you're living a life filled with joy and enjoying every moment of it. Remember, joy is more of a decision than it is a feeling. The angels of God make us aware of the joy of the Lord, which, in turn, becomes a supernatural strength—even when it comes to developing godly relationships.

The Angel of Covenant Promise

Last summer, while ministering at Calvary Pentecostal Campground, I became aware of an unusual angel who appeared to be fluttering and flowing like a worship flag in the middle of the tabernacle. This angel had wings like a robe and was enveloped by a multicolored rainbow that was glimmering and shimmering all around and within it. It has been difficult for me to explain what I saw because it was all so supernatural.

I saw this angel hovering halfway up one aisle, and when I asked the Lord about it, He said it was an angel of covenant promise. After the meeting that night, I reflected on everything that had happened, and I realized that the entire service had been orchestrated around the promises of God in the Scriptures.

At one point, I had asked those who were single and wanted to find a suitable mate to come forward. What is marriage all about? Is it not *covenant?* There was a couple in attendance who had been living together for many years but, for one reason or another, had never committed themselves through marriage. God spoke to their hearts that night, and they decided to get married as soon as possible. I came to the conclusion that God had been dealing with all of us about our covenant relationship with Him.

There were many facets of the revelation we received that night. God gave me a part of it, and we flowed in that part, and it was so very wonderful. This is one of the reasons God sends angels of divine love, to help us keep our covenants and to encourage married couples to love one another as they should.

Love One Another

In our marriage, Janet and I have learned how important it is to encourage one another. It is essential to see the treasure that God has placed within your spouse. Instead of focusing on any negatives, look for the positive things that cause you to flourish together. Then, it is vital to communicate positive, uplifting words to your spouse. Make this a daily habit. Tell your spouse how much you love him or her and how thankful you are for his or her presence in your life. When you do this, notice how the atmosphere begins to change in your home.

Let God lead you in speaking kind, affirming, positive blessings and scriptural promises over your spouse and your marriage. Remember, angels are always waiting to hear God's Word being spoken from your lips, and that's what sets them in motion. Our spiritual mentors, Charles and Frances Hunter, told us that when they woke up in the morning, they would kiss each other a hundred times before getting out of bed. What a great idea!

God's love is the best love, and when we share God's love with each other, it makes everything wonderful! Janet and I purpose to begin every day together in love, and end every day in the same way. The Scriptures warn us: *"Do not let the sun go down while you are still angry, and do not give the devil a foothold"* (Ephesians 4:26–27 NIV). In other words, never go to bed upset with each other. Make sure that the lines of communication in your marriage are always open. This is one of the ways in which angels of divine love will help you: keeping the atmosphere clear for connection, conversation, and communion with each other.

Discuss your feelings with your spouse, but also make time to hear and really understand his or her feelings. Be willing to repent if you've made a mistake, and be quick to forgive each other. Living in this way ensures that you won't give any room to the devil. Instead, you will make room for your angels of divine love to work.

Learning to Flow Together

Janet and I have learned how to flow together, especially when it comes to ministry. Some have asked us, "How can you work all the time with your spouse? Don't you need time apart? Doesn't it drive you crazy to always be together?" We can honestly answer that we are only crazy in love. We love spending every minute of every day with each other. We are not only a husband-and-wife team; we are also passionate lovers, ministry partners, and best friends. We are one. Bringing our different giftings and anointings together has made us complete and has allowed us to have a more dynamic ministry. We appreciate our differences and the unique perspective God has given each of us.

As we find ourselves individually in Christ, we discover our full potential together as a team. God wants you to learn how to flow together with Him, so that you can flow together as a couple. You can also learn to flow together with the angels that have been assigned to your life, your marriage, and your ministry.

Receiving Blessings Through Agreement and Priority

Do two walk together unless they have agreed to do so?

(Amos 3:3 NIV)

Agreement with divine order releases divine blessings. I have discovered this in my own marriage, family life, and ministry. First and foremost, God is my number one priority, and my immediate family is my number one ministry. I have made His purposes my purposes, and I desire to live my life yielded to His perfect will. It is through my intimate relationship with Christ that everything else I need or want flows, and this includes the ministry of angels. We will each be able to experience the ministry of angels only to the degree that we allow ourselves to intimately connect with Jesus Christ Himself.

Tragically, some people have tried to connect with their angels apart from Christ. That's a dangerous thing to attempt and can lead, instead, to being deceived by familiar, demonic spirits. Why would you want to seek a blessing more than you seek the One from whom all blessings flow? When we get our priorities right, everything else will come into perfect alignment. When we put God first, everything else follows in rightful succession.

Three Things That Hinder Angels of Divine Love

I've often been asked, "What hinders angels of divine love from working within people's lives and marriages?" I've noticed three predominant areas as common threads when speaking with people who are suffering in this way:

1. A lack of spending time together in God's Word.

2. A lack of praying together as a couple.

3. A lack of generously sharing intimate time together.

Ultimately, it comes down to a lack of true intimacy with each other and with God. I've discovered that the same things that activate the work of angels in our lives (speaking God's Word, prayer, and generosity) are also the things that hinder the activity of angels when and if they are neglected. It's been said, "The couple that prays together stays together," and that's really true. Everything flows from the top downward. When your priorities are set straight, you will have an abundance of love and angels who surround you continuously!

If you're ready to start *Seeing Angels*, let's pray:

Father, thank You for always wanting what is best for me. I am learning how to trust You more and more. I ask You to send Your angels of divine love right now. Allow them to be active in my life. Help my eyes to be open to see love, help my ears to be open to hear love, help my mouth to be open to speak love, and help my soul to be open to receive love.

Thank You for protecting me and keeping me safe. Thank You for guarding my heart against loss. Thank You for healing me from past disappointments and for allowing me to radiate Your love everywhere I go. As I put You first in my life, I know that all of Your goodness will fill my heart. In the loving name of Jesus, amen!

6

Angels on Extraordinary Assignment

In the same way, there is joy in the presence of God's angels
when even one sinner repents.
Luke 15:10 (NLT)

Janet and I have now been to more than seventy-five nations of the world, where we have seen God do many amazing miracles. Still, one of the most exciting things we have experienced is the salvation of lost souls. Whether we're ministering one-on-one or in a large gospel crusade, every time someone makes a decision for Christ, it's a time of great rejoicing! Many times, as we've had the privilege to open the altars for salvation, I've seen in the spirit hundreds, if not thousands, of angels gathering around us to celebrate sinners being washed clean by the blood of Jesus. Nothing excites or intrigues angels more than the winning of souls! It's true! Angels rejoiced in the day of your salvation too!

If you want to see, sense, and engage with more angels, win more souls for Christ! An atmosphere of salvation is always an atmosphere of angelic activation. Not only do angels come to rejoice in the moment of decision, but, during that time, God assigns new angels to work with every new believer as well.

I remember seeing this happen during an altar call while we were ministering in Lima, Peru, as many people were committing their lives to Jesus

Christ for the first time. Angels began swirling around the room and, immediately, creative miracles, signs, and wonders began breaking out. People reported being healed from long-term sicknesses, while others had supernatural oil and golden glory supernaturally appear on their hands—a sign of God's favor and blessing upon their lives. I've seen the same thing happen in Finland, Sweden, Poland, South Africa, Thailand, Australia, and many other nations. Angels love to celebrate the finished work of Christ!

An Angel Says, "Happy Birthday!"

Something supernatural happened to me not long ago during the month of May. As I was just waking up but still in a dreamy state, I saw and heard an angel wishing me "Happy Birthday," which was odd because my birthday is in January. I immediately sensed the angel was referring to my spiritual birthday. Again, this was unusual because I have never actually known when my spiritual birthday was. I remember my teacher the year I was saved, Mademoiselle Bouchard. But she was my teacher for both the first and second grade. Plus, as a young child, I never paid much attention to specific days, weeks, or months of the year. So the precise time of my salvation had always been a mystery to me.

But God knew my heart. He knew how important it was to me to know my spiritual birthday. I had never asked God to reveal it—doing so had never occurred to me—but He knew it was my heart's desire. So on that beautiful spring morning, He sent an angel to wish me a happy spiritual birthday. I know some of you may think this sounds crazy, but I am so thrilled and excited to finally know this! The angel said, "Happy Birthday!"

Later that same morning, I asked my son Lincoln to check the Internet to find out what day May 11 was in 1986 and 1987—my first and second grade years. It turns out that it was a Sunday in 1986. Yes! It was a Sunday night when I went down to the altar at Faith Tabernacle Church and gave my heart and life to the Lord. This was another confirmation. I was in the first grade that year. I called my parents to tell them what happened to me and, as I was speaking to my mom, my dad overheard and shouted, "Yes! It was in the month of May!" It's amazing that he remembered this but had never shared this with me before! I never knew the exact day, month, or year, but God confirmed it all to me through the voice of an angel!

Another amazing part of this story, is that although I clearly saw and heard the angel, I couldn't now tell you what he looked or sounded like. I can't remember any of that! But I guess the angel wasn't the focus. He was simply the delivery agent for my Happy Birthday-greeting from heaven.

It's so exciting to know that God loves to celebrate these special occasions, and that He's dispatched extraordinary angels on assignment because He cares about every detail of our lives. All of our children have also experienced the involvement of angels and have been similarly blessed by them. Angels often show up in ways we least expect. In fact, it has sometimes been in ways in which we didn't even know angels *could* act. We all have a lot to learn in this respect.

An Unexpected Surprise

Many years ago, we were to go to Indonesia for ministry. Janet asked me several times to call the airlines and confirm what time our flight was leaving the day after Christmas. I felt sure it was six in the evening, so I told her not to worry about it. On Christmas day, we were having dinner with my sister and her family, and Janet again asked me to call, saying that she just wanted to be sure. As before, I insisted that I knew the time. "We are leaving at six tomorrow evening," I told her. "We have plenty of time to get ready. Relax!"

For some reason, Janet was not satisfied. "No," she insisted, "you need to call them to be sure." So, I placed the call.

I had to wait on the line for the longest time. When an operator finally answered and I asked about the departure time, she looked it up and then said, "Sir, your flight is leaving at six in the morning." I suddenly felt all of the blood rush out of my body.

By then, it was close to midnight and we had all the mess from Christmas morning still waiting at our house and all the Christmas decorations still up. We would need to buy some diapers and clothes for Lincoln (who was only two at the time), plus we had to pack everything up. I remember thinking, *There is no way we can get all of this done, get some rest, and get to the airport so early.*

There was another important consideration: Janet and I both like to keep our home neat and clean, so we try to leave it that way when we go away on any trip, so that it will be that way when we get back. That wasn't going to be possible this time. We quickly got ready and flew to Indonesia, leaving the house a mess for the many weeks we were to be away.

We had a wonderful time in Indonesia, but as we were coming back, I remember thinking that I was not looking forward to arriving to a messy house. Just taking down the Christmas decorations and returning everything to normal was a job in itself. Ugh!

We finally got home, and when we walked in the door, we were amazed. Everything had been put away exactly where it was supposed to be and the whole house had been cleaned. All of the Christmas decorations had been taken down and stored exactly where I liked to keep them. It was all too wonderful for words!

I thought my mother must have come over and cleaned, so I called to thank her. She was surprised and said she hadn't done it. "I'm sorry," she said, "I just didn't have time with all the activity of the holidays."

"Well, who could it have been?" I asked. And, of course, there was no answer.

Could it be possible that the Lord had sent an angel or angels to clean our house? Well, for sure He cares about every detail of our lives, there can be no doubt of that. He knows what is important to us and takes care of it. The more I thought about it, the surer I became that God had sent cleaning angels to take care of our mess.

But, again, was that possible? Well, God has healing angels, protecting angels, prosperity angels, and deliverance angels. Why not cleaning angels?

Angels to the Rescue

When we speak of all the supernatural things angels can do, I think it's essential to mention an important truth: the assignment of your angels is not to remove your own personal responsibility from any given situation, but rather to make what seems impossible *naturally* possible *supernaturally*. Angels are sent to us as ministering spirits, heavenly messengers, to partner with us in God's plans, purposes, and assignments for our life. But you should never expect an angel to do something that *you* can do.

THE ASSIGNMENT OF YOUR ANGELS IS NOT TO REMOVE YOUR OWN PERSONAL RESPONSIBILITY FROM ANY GIVEN SITUATION, BUT RATHER TO MAKE WHAT SEEMS IMPOSSIBLE *NATURALLY* POSSIBLE *SUPERNATURALLY.*

If you *can* do a thing, then that's *your* responsibility. God doesn't send angels to us so we can be lazy. Actually, it's quite the contrary. He sends angels into our lives so that we will be much more efficient and effective in fulfilling our life mission. The angels of God are standing ready to intervene in our lives whenever we need them. When we say, "God, I'm at the end of my wits and don't know what to do or where to turn," that very moment, He has made angels available to us. Yes, even when we don't know how we're going to make it, He has angel ministers ready to act on our behalf.

David sang:

I sought the Lord, and he answered me; he delivered me from all my fears. Those who look to him are radiant; their faces are never covered with shame. This poor man called, and the Lord heard him; he saved him out of all his troubles. The angel of the Lord encamps around those who fear him, and he delivers them. (Psalm 34:4–7 NIV)

Notice what David said: "*he answered me.*" God hears our prayers. He not only heard David, but he also delivered David from all of his fears. And God's promise is that "*the angel of the Lord encamps around those who fear him, and he delivers them.*" God's angels are not only ready to help us in the distresses of our daily lives, they are ever ready to aid and assist us in carrying out His purposes in all the earth.

I was telling someone the testimony of the cleaning angel, and they said, "Brother Joshua, we don't believe it was angels that cleaned your house." They had never heard of such a thing and were trying to tell me all the reasons it couldn't happen.

I answered, "You know what assured me that it was an angel?" It was a rhetorical question, and I didn't give them time to answer, but went on, "It was that everything was put away in the containers I always keep it in. Nobody else on earth, except me, knows how I want all our Christmas decorations to be put away, and yet, it was all put away exactly as I wanted it. God did a perfect work."

When I shared this testimony in a meeting, an elderly lady came up to me and said, "Well, I need my house painted, and I don't have the strength, money, or ability to do it. Do you think God has painting angels?"

I said, "I don't know. Let's pray about it."

We prayed, and the lady came back later and said, "My house has been painted, and I can't explain it. When I woke up in the morning, it was done. So it's true; God has painting angels."

I shared this testimony with one of my spiritual mothers, "Momma" Billie Deck, in Springfield, Virginia, and she said, "We have a plumbing problem in our basement. The roots of the trees outside have grown right into the drain pipes in our basement, so I guess we need plumbing angels."

I said, "Well, let's just release them." Sure enough, without her ever seeing their activity, those angels came and took the tree roots out of the drain. Momma Billie contacted me and told me that the plumbing problem had been completely resolved. Praise God!

Isn't that amazing! God has many types of angels. I'm sure this all sounds very strange to some people. If it seems strange to you, just take it to the Lord in prayer and see what He tells you about it.

An Angel Bakes a Power Cake

Throughout the Scriptures, we see angels at work in the lives of God's people to strengthen them. One such angel appeared to Elijah and baked him a cake, giving him supernatural food to eat. This power cake became strength for the journey ahead of him. The Scriptures show that this "angel food" enabled Elijah to travel, strengthened in this miraculous way, for forty days and forty nights, until he reached Mount Sinai:

> *Then he lay down and slept under the broom tree. But as he was sleeping, an angel touched him and told him, "Get up and eat!" He looked around and there beside his head was some bread baked on hot stones and a jar of water! So he ate and drank and lay down again. Then the angel of the LORD came again and touched him and said, "Get up and eat some more, or the journey ahead will be too much for you." So he got up and ate and drank, and the food gave him enough strength to travel forty days and forty nights to Mount Sinai, the mountain of God.*
> (1 Kings 19:5–8 NLT)

Angels Strengthen Us in New Zealand

Several years ago, the Lord sent Janet and me, along with a team, to the North Island of New Zealand to minister. We spent almost a month there, releasing the glory of God in numerous churches and other locations. This was an exciting adventure, as we were experiencing the tangible presence of God in every single meeting. During this ministry trip, the Lord began revealing the reality of His angels to us in a brand new way.

About halfway through our month-long stay in New Zealand, some of those on the ministry team began to feel weary in their bodies due to the demanding travel and tight ministry schedule we were maintaining. One night, after a church meeting in a place called Manakau, we returned to our hotel room to find that angels had been activated on our behalf to minister God's strengthening power to our physical bodies. The Lord had sent an angel who brought us golden leaves from the trees in heaven. We were astonished to find these delicate leaves beautifully placed on the open pages of one of our Bibles.

While we were in a state of awe over this manifestation, the Spirit of God began to give us instructions by revealing to one of the team members that these golden leaves were meant to be an edible source of strength and supernatural empowerment. Just as Elijah had eaten the cake provided by angels, we began to partake of this heavenly substance, and as we ate the miraculous golden leaves so wonderfully provided, they gave strength and wholeness to our bodies. The next day, because of our newfound strength, we were able to travel by foot, along with the rest of the ministry team, on a round-trip trek to the top of Mount Rangitoto. What a miracle it was!

We continued ministering for the rest of our appointed schedule in New Zealand with supernatural strength and vigor through the empowerment we had received from the Lord. We rejoiced and thanked our Lord Jesus Christ, for He had allowed us to encounter His strengthening touch in a new way. God chose to release this experience to us through the remarkable ministry of His angels.

The Finding Angels

I believe that all of God's angels work to bring us into the blessing that He has provided through the finished work of Christ, but there seem to be some angels who are charged with the specific task of helping us to find treasured things that have gone missing. I believe that these are our guardian angels, the ones who watch over us on a continual basis. They also serve as "finding angels," because they care about every important detail of our lives.

When we ask God for His help, these angels get to work, assisting us to find whatever has been lost. This can include personal keepsakes that hold sentimental value (jewelry, photos, etc.), misplaced files or documents, missing household items, inheritances, and even lost people. I witnessed these angels firsthand when Janet and I took our first trip to Israel.

Soon after landing in Israel, we discovered that our luggage had not arrived on the same plane. Somehow, it had been delayed, and the airline said it would arrive the following day. It didn't arrive the next day either. The problem was that we were on a tour of the Holy Land, and each day, we stayed at a different hotel in a different location. We called the airline and notified them of our itinerary, but somehow our luggage still wasn't reaching us.

Several days into our trip, discouragement set in. All we wanted was to put on some fresh clothes, but that was not possible. That day, we went on an all-day tour. When we arrived back at the hotel that night and checked with the front desk, hoping against hope that something had changed, all they had was a note from the airline stating that our luggage had still not arrived. They apologized and tried to comfort us the best they could.

At this point, Janet was so tired of wearing the same clothes over and over that her eyes now filled with tears. As we were getting on the elevator, I did my best to console her. Another person on the elevator, after overhearing our conversation, offered this advice: "Why don't you just ask your angels to bring the luggage to you?" Wow! Why hadn't we thought of that? This was something my mother had taught us to do ever since we were small children. Whenever we would lose something or discover that something had gone missing, she would tell us: "Pray, and ask God to help you find it"—and He always did. The folks on the elevator quickly prayed for us, and we agreed, asking God to release those finding angels to bring us our lost luggage.

We got off the elevator and walked down the hallway to our room. When we opened the door, there in front of us were our two pieces of lost luggage! We could hardly believe our eyes. Did the hotel personnel make a mistake by telling us that the luggage had not yet arrived, or had angels gone and quickly retrieved our suitcases for us? I will always believe that angels were involved.

Several years ago, one of my friends frantically called me on the phone. She had been hosting a visiting guest in her home in Tampa, Florida, and they had spent the week visiting many different tourist destinations, taking photos, and making great memories together. The reason for the frantic phone call was that she had left her camera on a table at a restaurant where they had been eating, and when they went back to get it, someone had already removed it from the table. Either it had gone missing or been stolen. Either way, she was devastated because the camera held all the photos and memories from that entire week. She said, "Joshua, is it possible for God to send angels to find my camera?"

I replied, "Yes, absolutely!"

With renewed confidence, she asked, "Can we ask God to release those angels now?" That's what we did. When we pray to God, He authorizes His angels to go to work on our behalf. This shouldn't be difficult for anyone. You can pray something as simple as this: "Heavenly Father, please help me to find _____. Release Your finding angels to bring it to me now, in Jesus's name."

It wasn't long before my friend called me back with the most outrageous testimony:

> I called my daughter who was at home doing laundry. While we were speaking, she suddenly noticed that my camera was sitting on top of a pile of clothes in her laundry basket. I asked her to turn it on and verify that it was indeed my camera. Sure enough, the last pictures taken were those photos in the restaurant where my friend and I had eaten.

How did that camera get from a restaurant across town to a pile of laundry in her daughter's house? It doesn't make any sense at all. But these things don't need to make sense. We just need to thank God and trust that His angels are working on our behalf.

Finding angels are available for you too! Begin working with them. It's fun to see your angels returning your missing items to places where you are certain you never left them. One lady got back a missing family heirloom that had been lost for ten years! Jesus said, *"Ask, and it shall be given you"* (Matthew 7:7).

When we are driving through an overcrowded parking lot, we ask God to send His angels to find us a perfect parking space. And it works! Sometimes that perfect parking space is up front, close to the buildings, and we're thankful for it. At other times, that perfect parking space is at the back of the lot, and we realize that God is giving us an opportunity to exercise and remain healthy! We rejoice in both situations! God always knows best.

If you're ready to start *Seeing Angels*, let's pray:

> Heavenly Father, You are so good. You never cease to amaze me with all that You do. Your ways are perfect and so much better than my ways. Thank You for the supernatural surprises that You release in my life through the ministry assignments of Your angels. I am amazed at all of Your extraordinary miracles that fill my life. In the wonder-working name of Jesus, amen!

7

Angels of Breakthrough and Revival

But the angel of the Lord by night opened the prison doors,
and brought them forth.
Acts 5:19

There are angels of breakthrough, and I'm sure that you could use their intervention in your life. Breakthrough angels minister to us in the realms of personal health, finances, and family situations. They intervene for ministries, businesses, and workplace and school situations, and they often produce sudden reversals in dire circumstances. Like all other angels, they can take on many different appearances, as the Spirit allows. Expect it and rejoice in it.

Fireballs of Breakthrough in Victoria, British Columbia

Several years ago, while ministering in Canada, we experienced a great outpouring of God's Spirit and healing power. People were healed of Alzheimer's disease, mental illness, and depression, as well as neck, back, and joint pain. Red blood cells were recreated in the bodies of those who needed them. In addition, stomach and digestive problems were cured, lumps and cysts dissolved, and hips, shoulders, and ankles were touched by the divine healing flow. Deaf ears were also opened, and sight was restored to the blind. Many people also received great financial miracles as they sowed generously into the open-heaven atmosphere present in those meetings!

During this time of great outpouring, I had another unusual encounter with an angel in my hotel room. This angel reached into the air, grabbed hold of a flaming fireball, and then threw it at me. As he threw it, he shouted, "*Catch!*" Amazingly, I did!

As soon as I caught that flaming fireball in my hands, it exploded and, all around me, there was a golden glory. Then the angel said, "Get ready to catch; more miracles are coming!" After that encounter, my entire body vibrated under the power of God for the next several hours. It felt as though there were waves of electricity pulsating through me.

While I was preaching the following day, this same angel appeared at the back of the sanctuary and proceeded to pull down a fireball from heaven and throw it at me. In order to catch it, I had to leap from behind the pulpit, race over to the left side of the sanctuary, and reach over the heads of the people seated there. It was wild! Somehow I did it. As soon as I caught that fireball, it exploded as before, once again spreading golden glory all over my hands, arms, and face, as well as on those who were sitting beneath the explosion. That fireball was also filled with words of knowledge that blessed many people in attendance.

It is impossible to put into words the powerful and tangible weight of the glory of God we experienced that night. Here is Pastor Susan McLean's firsthand account:

> People traveled from Salmon Arm, Prince George, and other cities to attend the Days of Glory meetings with Joshua Mills in Victoria, and they were not disappointed. Visible manifestations of God's glory occurred in all the meetings, with a deluge of golden dust on the last night. An angel met Joshua at the door of his hotel room the night before and threw him a fiery ball of glory. The next night the same angel appeared in the meeting and threw him fiery balls of glory. The people in the meeting did not see the angel, but many saw and heard Joshua run forward to catch the balls that then exploded in the air. It was awe-inspiring to see manifestations of the supernatural come into the natural realm!

Joshua went into the crowd, touching people on their foreheads and praying for them, and everywhere, people were plastered with golden dust. As we received testimonies, both during and after the week of meetings, we saw that a few moments in the glory can change people's lives forever. People were healed from longstanding painful conditions, even as they walked into the meetings and while worshiping. People who had struggled for years with bad habits like smoking were suddenly free. One lady was completely delivered from a lifetime of shame and intimidation from childhood sexual abuse. Another was set free from years of depression and battles with thoughts of suicide. Several people received dramatic financial blessings too!

Those meetings were so exciting and so many miracles were released, but that's what happens when God sends angels of breakthrough. Every time we pray and speak the Word of God boldly, angels are released in accordance with that Word. Let go of all resistance, all anxiety, and all fear, and begin to cooperate with heaven's purposes. If you need a breakthrough in your life right now, begin speaking God's Word of breakthrough.

Although Peter was securely locked up in prison, we can see in the Bible what happened when the church began to pray and speak with faith:

Suddenly an angel of the Lord appeared and a light shone in the cell. He struck Peter on the side and woke him up. "Quick, get up!" he said, and the chains fell off Peter's wrists.   (Acts 12:7 NIV)

"*Suddenly,*" a breakthrough angel appeared in Peter's prison cell. This means that Peter wasn't necessarily expecting it at that particular moment in time. The appearance of the angel was unexpected. It all happened in an instant. When we have been going through something for a long time and God moves to release us, the release seems sudden. You might be thinking you will have to go through this thing for many more weeks, months, or even years. Some trials drag on for decades. But God delights in bringing us His "suddenlies." "*Suddenly an angel of the Lord appeared.*" Believe for it in your life too!

The angel who came to Peter had to wake him up. As Peter came out of sleep, there was a strange light in his cell, and he saw a stranger standing before him, saying, *"Quick, get up!"* Next, the chains were falling from his wrists. It all happened so *suddenly*.

When your angel of breakthrough gives you instructions from heaven, don't resist and don't hold back. Move immediately in obedience to those instructions, and do whatever the angel is telling you to do.

Maybe some do not yet know that God sends angels with divine instructions. He sends angels to direct preachers and ministries. He sends angels with ministry assignments. (See Acts 8:26.) In the past, people have warned me never to say that. "Don't you realize," they say, "that some have gotten into error because they listened to the message of an angel." Well, that would not have been a real angel. God's angels bring His messages, and their words will always line up perfectly with His written Word. They will bring a confirmation of the things that God has already been revealing to you by His Spirit.

A Breakthrough Angel in Sonora, California

Several years ago, we were ministering at meetings near Yosemite National Park in California. One night, another minister spoke. He was just passing through town, but he told us about a unique thing that had happened in his life. An angel named Breakthrough had been assigned to travel with him and his ministry everywhere he went. This angel had been sent on specific assignment to prepare regions for revival.

This minister was not permitted to go just anywhere. He had to be sensitive to the leading of the Spirit and go where God directed him. As long as he did that, the angel accompanied him, and everywhere they went, spiritual breakthrough was released over people.

I personally witnessed this in the meetings. When Breakthrough began to minister, there was an outpouring of signs, wonders, and miracles. There was spiritual deliverance and deep conviction that came upon the people. Salvation was flowing freely in that place. It was awesome! This angel brought a message, saying, "Tell the people three words: *'Move, move, move!'* We'll be moving with those who move in the things of God!"

It doesn't matter how difficult a situation might seem in the natural, when a breakthrough angel comes, and you partner with that angel, something *will* break through. So get ready to expect this in your own life. Breakthrough angels have been released from heaven. Are you willing to let them work in you?

Angels of Harvest

There are also angels of harvest, some who reap on their own and others who assist us in the harvest. John the Revelator wrote about them:

> *Then another angel came out of the temple and called in a loud voice to him who was sitting on the cloud, "Take your sickle and reap, because the time to reap has come, for the harvest of the earth is ripe."*
> (Revelation 14:15 NIV)

In these last days, we have a great responsibility at hand. We have been commissioned by Jesus to go into all the earth, proclaiming the Good News of the gospel and reaping a harvest of the nations. We can't do this on our own, nor does God expect us to. Are you willing to learn how to work with the angels of harvest? They are available for you.

In her book, *A Divine Revelation of Heaven*, Mary K. Baxter shared about a time when angels of harvest were moving in a church where she was ministering:

> When it was time for the altar call, I saw angels going among the congregation, nudging people to go to the altar and give their hearts to the Lord. When I saw the angels touching the hearts of individuals, the blackest sins began to churn up and out of their hearts as they knelt and prayed to God. Oh, it was beautiful!
>
> In my spirit, I could see chains that were wrapped around the people. As people received forgiveness, angels seemed to break the bondage, to shatter the chains, to cast them off. The bands broke as people began to raise their hands and confess their sins to the Lord.
>
> Cries and shouts went up everywhere from souls who had been delivered.[22]

22. Mary K. Baxter, *A Divine Revelation of Heaven* (New Kensington, PA: Whitaker House, 1998), 164–165.

When we cooperate with God's angels, the positive results are amazing! It doesn't matter what things look like in the natural, you can reap a great harvest when you work with harvesting angels. Embrace them and work with them.

Angels Work With Us

Quite a few years ago, as I was traveling to minister in Camuy, Puerto Rico, while I was still on the airplane, high in the sky, the Spirit began to show me some things regarding the angels who are assigned to our ministry. At this point, I was already familiar with my personal angels (understanding their function for both my own personal life and ministry), but I hadn't yet given much thought to the angels specifically assigned to International Glory Ministries. The Lord began to show me that everywhere we went, assigned angels went with us.

The angels who go with us make up a large company, and they themselves are large, standing from twelve to twenty feet tall. While I'm ministering, people will often tell me that they see one or more of these angels standing behind me. They are usually seen as a silhouette with a white or golden glow. Although these angels accompany me to each ministry assignment, God has shown me that they don't necessarily accompany me back home. Instead, they remain in that place long after I have left. It is for this reason that supernatural manifestations and demonstrations continue to take place long after I've gone home.

I've seen in the Spirit that, as I minister, these angels are watching to see who among the crowd is willing to receive the Word, those who diligently pursue these matters in personal prayer and intercession and those who are inclined to open themselves fully to the purposes of God. When the angels find such a person, they are released from our ministry and stay in that location, to continue working with people there to bring forth the manifestation of what has been spoken.

I shared this revelation with the church in Camuy, and the people were determined to passionately pursue the things of God. Therefore, after we left, the miracles continued to flow with ease. Pastor Tito later sent an email in which he reported:

We keep receiving testimonies from the meetings, like the mechanic angels who fixed the flat tire on a lady's car and people receiving money miracles. There is a girl who needed a root canal and received a dental miracle.

God wants His glory and miracles to surround us continually, so He has provided the assistance of His angels, but we must be willing to work with them. If the person an angel is assigned to becomes complacent, that angel will go looking for someone more willing to passionately pursue the things of God.

An Atmosphere Shift in Singapore

We have another big angel, one who continually watches over our ministry. He also has a whole host of angels who work with him. This angel is taller than I can even describe, and he has a full array of wings, with the largest white feathers I have ever seen. Each feather is probably at least ten feet in length. They are huge! When I see him, I am reminded of God's promise in Psalm 91:4, which says, *"He shall cover you with His feathers."* That's exactly what God does for us and our ministry through the service of this angel.

This angel is what I call an atmosphere angel, for one of his specific assignments is to help us "hold open" the atmosphere of glory wherever we go. This makes it easy for me to minister in the glory. I don't need to fast for forty days each time in order to enter in, and it's never a painstaking ordeal. Wherever I go, the glory is released with ease. Even in the most difficult regions, and under the most troublesome situations, we have still experienced the visitation of the glory of God.

For example, I was invited to minister in an Anglican church in Singapore, and when I arrived, the pastor informed me that he didn't believe in divine healing, the current reality of miracles, or God's ability to prosper His people. *Then why was I invited to come here?* I was wondering.

I soon learned that, technically, this pastor had *not* invited me. Between the time I had received the invitation and the time I arrived, the former pastor (the one who was Spirit-filled and had initially invited me) had retired and the church had inducted a new pastor, one who didn't believe in the things of the Spirit. In the natural, this would have been an impossible situation, but thank God, *"all things are possible to him that believes"* (Mark 9:23), and I believe!

I would be lying if I told you that I didn't feel stressed out or anxious at that moment; I did. I didn't know how I would make it through an entire weekend of ministry in such a restrictive atmosphere. Thank God for His angels! I hadn't yet met the large angel who watches over our ministry, and I wasn't yet aware of his ministry function, but I can tell you that I surely felt his presence with me during those days. In spite of the pastor and his preconceived ideas of what could and could not happen, miracles happened, healings took place, and supernatural finances were released. In those services, God did everything that pastor didn't believe in! Isn't God wonderful?

God has assigned this angel to our ministry, and he serves the purposes of God that we are called to. Very often, someone will comment to me: "I can feel the glory whenever you minister, and it feels so different than anything else I've experienced in my life." That lets me know that God's angels are working with us so that we can fulfill our calling. I am called to change the atmosphere everywhere I go. This is something our ministry has become well known for, and God has given us His angels to help us make it happen.

An Angel Named Swift

My friend, Patricia King, has an angel named Swift who is assigned to her prophetic ministry, and Swift's name perfectly describes what he does. He brings acceleration to God-given assignments, helping to carry the ministry forward. Patricia has told me that when God sent Swift to her, everything accelerated, from the time of revelation to the time of implementation, and that acceleration continues to this day.

Swift takes on the appearance of a brown and golden eagle. He has gold talons, wing tips, and a beak. This makes sense in the Spirit, since eagles represent accurate or "eagle-eye" vision, and also the strength and ability to carry the people of God forward (see Exodus 19:4; Deuteronomy 32:11), and gold prophetically represents the glory of God (see Exodus 25:11), the glory that brings divine acceleration without limitation.

The Bible describes how Philip had an angel appear to him, to help bring direction to his ministry:

And the angel of the Lord spoke to Philip, saying, Arise, and go toward the south to the way that goes down from Jerusalem to Gaza, which is desert. (Acts 8:26)

God is able to send the ministry of His breakthrough and revival angels to us in many different forms. Sometimes they come in the most unusual and supernatural ways!

Supernatural Oil, Angel Voices, and Heavenly Music

I had been invited as one of the speaking guests at Dr. A. L. and Joyce Gill's annual Mountain Top Encounter, in Big Bear Lake, California. From the time I arrived on the property, I could feel the swirling of angels all around us. I knew that they were ministering spirits and that the Lord had sent them to minister to everyone present at the meetings. God spoke two words to my spirit: "intensified...glory." And that's exactly what happened in those days!

After our meeting that first night, I had a dream in which I saw an angel tipping a huge golden bowl toward the earth. The bowl was filled with a golden oil, and that oil was being poured out all over the world. The Bible reveals that this oil is, in fact, the prayers of the saints:

And when He had taken the book, the four beasts and four and twenty elders fell down before the Lamb, having every one of them harps, and golden vials full of odors, which are the prayers of saints.
(Revelations 5:8)

God was pouring out the answers to prayers as a blessing to the earth.

I woke up from the dream and looked at the clock. It was 2:35 in the morning. I quickly noticed that my head, my hands, and my feet were all dripping with oil. Later, I connected this message with Psalm 23:5, which says that God *"anoint[s] my head with oil"*! It seemed clear that He was taking me into a deeper spiritual encounter, so I turned on the bedside lamp and began worshiping Him.

When I looked up from my bed, I noticed that there were two cups placed on a long table at the foot of the bed. I knew those hadn't been there when I went to sleep, and they were full, in fact, running over, with supernatural oil. Also, my Bible was laid open between the two cups. I remembered specifically that before I went to bed, I had placed that Bible on the top of a tall entertainment cabinet in the room. Somehow, it had been moved. I instantly knew that angels had been at work in my hotel room, even while I was sleeping and having a heavenly dream.

I got up to touch and smell the oil, and I noticed that the open pages of my Bible were covered in a sparkling golden substance. I reached out, with my oil-soaked hands, to wipe one of the pages and saw that it was opened to Revelation 5. This was a confirmation of the dream. God was causing it to manifest in my very room.

I didn't know it, but the worship leader, who was staying in the next room, was seeing lights flashing and bouncing around his room all night long. This was another manifestation of the angels at work. I couldn't go back to sleep, so I stayed up for hours, worshiping the Lord in the atmosphere that filled my room.

The next morning, I carried the cups of supernatural oil to the meeting, expecting that we would use it to anoint everyone in that early session, but before I could finish my message, the supernatural oil began to flow again from my hands. This time, it was so profuse that everyone who had gathered could see it. It was dripping off of my hands and running down my arms.

I asked everyone in attendance to form a prayer line around the perimeter of the room, so that I could lay hands on each of them and bless them with the heavenly oil that was being poured out. As I began to lay hands on the people, miracles began happening instantaneously. Some received healing in their physical bodies. Others received emotional and spiritual breakthroughs.

Eventually, the worship leader became so overwhelmed by the presence of God in the room that he took his hands off of the keyboard, but when he did, the music didn't stop. It continued to play.

I later confirmed that this music had not been prerecorded or pre-programmed. What was happening was so supernatural that the worship leader fell to the floor, overcome by the power of the Spirit. Still, the keyboard continued to play heavenly sounds.

After a while, the voices of angels could be heard, singing along with the spontaneous heavenly music. That day marked a new beginning of out-pouring all over the world, and people in many places entered into a new season of revival.

If you're ready to start *Seeing Angels,* let's pray:

Heavenly Father, I'm filled with great faith and supernatural anticipation for Your angels of breakthrough and revival to move on my behalf. Thank You for assigning them over my life. I choose to move with these angels. I agree with them, and I will work with them to see breakthrough and revival increase around me everywhere I go. In Jesus's powerful name, amen!

8

Angels over Churches, Cities, and Nations

And I saw another angel fly in the midst of heaven, having the everlasting gospel to preach to them that dwell on the earth, and to every nation, and kindred, and tongue, and people.
Revelation 14:6

We've already seen in the Bible that angels have been assigned over our personal lives, but did you realize that there are also angels assigned over your church, your city, and your nation? It's true.

Yes, there are angels specifically assigned to help in the work of the ministry. They partner with apostles, prophets, evangelists, and teachers. There are also angels specifically assigned to individual churches. These angels oversee ministry concerns, finances, and church assignments, and they desire to help local pastors succeed in their calling. Sometimes these angels are assigned to bring a specific word or direction to the church they are called to. We see these angels mentioned in the book of Revelation:

+ *"the angel of the church of Ephesus"* (Revelation 2:1)

+ *"the angel of the church in Smyrna"* (Revelation 2:8)

+ *"the angel of the church in Pergamos"* (Revelation 2:12)

+ *"the angel of the church in Thyatira"* (Revelation 2:18)

+ *"the angel of the church in Sardis"* (Revelation 3:1)

+ *"the angel of the church in Philadelphia"* (Revelation 3:7)

+ *"the angel of the church of the Laodiceans"* (Revelation 3:14)

Because the Greek word *angelos* means "messenger," some theologians have struggled with this supernatural idea, proposing instead that these "messengers" may just have been pastors or bishops over the church. Are these messengers human? Or could it be possible for heavenly messengers to watch over individual churches? We see John clearly answering this question by precisely stating:

> *The mystery of the seven stars which you saw in My right hand, and the seven golden candlesticks. The seven stars are the angels of the seven churches: and the seven candlesticks which you saw are the seven churches.*
>
> (Revelation 1:20)

Historic British theologian J. B. Lightfoot explained it this way:

> This contrast between the heavenly and the earthly fires—the star shining steadily by its own inherent eternal light, and the lamp flickering and uncertain, requiring to be fed with fuel and tended with care—cannot be devoid of meaning. The star is the suprasensual counterpart, the heavenly representative; the lamp, the earthly realization, the outward embodiment.[23]

I believe that God used the apostle John, while he was exiled on the isle of Patmos, to write messages addressed to these seven angels. Then the angels would take the messages and share them with the respective church congregations. It is also significant to note that John emphasized how important it was for the church to *"hear what the Spirit says to the churches"* (repeated seven times in Revelation 2–3). These messages clearly were not *for* the angels; the angels were simply the delivery agents for God's message to be given to the churches.

---

23. J. B. Lightfoot, *The Christian Ministry* (New York: T. Whittaker, 1878), 73.

Also notice that the *"stars"* were held in Jesus's right hand. In the Scriptures, the right hand represents protection, guidance, strength, and victory. (See Exodus 15:6; Psalm 20:6, 98:1.) These are all attributes that God has given to our guardian angels. In the same way that we each have personal guardian angels, the Lord has made provision for each and every church to have a guardian angel.

It's interesting to note that the last words of Jesus recorded in the Bible were about the ministry of an angel in the church. In Revelation 22:16, he said: *"I Jesus have sent My angel to testify to you these things in the churches."*

These angels are there to help the pastor and the church members to fulfill their purposes as a congregation of believers.

The City of Angels

Los Angeles is known as "the city of angels." The name *Los Angeles*, in Spanish, literally means "the angels." I don't think it's a coincidence that God chose this physical location to birth the modern move of His Spirit at the turn of the twentieth century. Anytime God wants to show up and manifest Himself, His angels always seem to be involved. Look at the evidence we can find for this in the Scriptures:

+ God created the earth in the atmosphere of angelic hosts singing His praises. (See Job 38:4–7.)

+ An angel manifested in the midst of the fiery furnace, representing the victory of God's people. (See Daniel 3:13–29.)

+ An angel army set an ambush against the enemies of Israel, allowing Jehoshaphat and his men to win the war. (See 2 Chronicles 20:22.)

+ An angel told Zacharias that his wife, Elizabeth, would bear a son in her old age. (See Luke 1:13.)

+ An angel appeared to Mary to announce that she would conceive the Christ child. (See Luke 1:30–31.)

+ Angels descend from heaven to announce Christ's birth to the shepherds in the fields of Judea. (See Luke 2:9–14.)

+ Women, followers of Jesus, saw a vision of angels, who told them Jesus was alive. (See Luke 24:23.)

- ✦ Two angels dressed in white garments declared the return of Christ. (See Acts 1:10–11.)

- ✦ Angels of "wind" and "fire" prepared the atmosphere for the arrival of the Holy Spirit. (See Acts 2:2–4.)

There are many angels hovering over Los Angeles, waiting for those who will put their ministry service to use, and many angels are hovering over your city too! Do you believe it?

A few years ago, my friend Pastor Rick Wright went to a special meeting that was being held at the Bonnie Brae House (the initial location where the Azusa Street Revival began) near Westlake in Los Angeles. He said that as he walked into the worship service, he became extremely sensitive to the glorious atmosphere that was present, so much so that his body began to physically shake. Although he couldn't see an angel, he said that he could immediately feel the presence of a large angel that was standing on the property. Like a laser beam entering into his spirit, he received a message from that angel: "My name is Historic, I am the angel of Azusa Street, and I create history." God allowed him to know that this was one of the angels who preside over Los Angeles. Historic is believed to be a seraph, full of fire—that same revival fire that ignited the Azusa Street Revival to spread all over the world!

Actually, the earth has witnessed many historic revivals being birthed from the Los Angeles region, genuine moves of God that have changed history. On a prayer walk some time later, Pastor Rick saw a fallen angel who was presiding over Hollywood. It was a territorial spirit named Perverted Wisdom. This coincided with Isaiah 47:10, which says: *"For you have trusted in your wickedness: you have said, None sees me. Your wisdom and your knowledge, it has perverted you; and you have said in your heart, I am, and none else beside me."* This evil spirit attempts to infiltrate the earth with its perversions, all the while seeming brilliant, in order to corrupt history through Hollywood.

The first night I went to do some recording at Capitol Records in Hollywood, the team there took me up to the roof to get the "perfect view" of the L.A. skyline. Wow, did I ever get a view! Not only could I see across all the sparkling lights of Los Angeles, but in the spiritual realm, I could see a large angel who was standing atop the Capitol Records tower. He stood even higher than the needle atop that building. He had been sent there by God, as a holy angel who presides over music. Many of the people who were on the top of the roof that night could sense the presence of this angel. These are true supernatural realities, and this is the war that's being waged in the spirit world.

The Bible reminds us:

> For we wrestle not against flesh and blood, but against principalities, against powers, against the rulers of the darkness of this world, against spiritual wickedness in high places.   (Ephesians 6:12)

There are both holy and fallen angels who preside over regions, and the Scriptures tell us that they fight against one another. (See Revelation 12:7–10.) This is one of the reasons I have been teaching an Angel School on the backlot at Warner Brothers Studios in Burbank for the past few years. God's people need to understand more about angels and how to empower them over churches, cities, and nations through prayer, intercession, and decrees.

God Creates Boundaries and Sets Supervising Angels

> God Most High gave land to every nation. He assigned a guardian angel to each of them, but the LORD himself takes care of Israel.
>   (Deuteronomy 32:8–9 CEV)

God literally created boundary lines, and when He created separate nations in the earth, according to *The Living Bible*, "He gave each of them a supervising angel." When I began to study this passage of Scripture, I discovered that many modern Bible translations recognize the angelic nature of this verse:

+ "He made as many nations as there are angels" (ERV).

+ "He assigned to each nation a heavenly being" (GNT).

+ "He put each of the peoples within boundaries under the care of divine guardians" (MSG).

+ "He set the boundaries of the people, *according to the number of the heavenly assembly*" (NET).

+ "He established the boundaries of the peoples according to the number in his heavenly court" (NLT).

Nations were created around certain angelic rulers, angelic principalities, angelic dominions, and angelic powers. In other words, when an angel goes to war, the nation that angel represents also goes to war. The laborers in Christ's vineyard must understand the things that are happening in the spirit world. There is a spiritual influence that is creating the natural realities we can see in the flesh. What we are seeing is real enough, but it is emanating from a spiritual source. Paul wrote to the Ephesian believers:

> *Finally, my brethren, be strong in the Lord, and in the power of His might.*
>   (Ephesians 6:10)

This is a prophetic command to each of us. "*Be strong in the Lord, and in the power of his might.*" It continues in the next verses: "*Put on the whole armor of God, that you may be able to stand against the wiles of the devil*" (verse 11). Who is our enemy? It is the devil and his fallen angels, and we must be able to stand against his plans, his assignments, and his attacks. We must stand and take our place in the kingdom of God. Why? "*For we wrestle not against flesh and blood*" (verse 12). Oh, if we could just stay in the glory! That's the very best place to be. That's where you will learn to work with your angels. That's the place where you can learn to rest in the loving arms of Jesus, knowing that He is the Prince of Peace. God is looking for someone who will be willing to get into the glory and push things through by His Spirit. He is looking for true believers.[24]

In Daniel's time, the Jewish people were held captive, oppressed by the Persian Empire. Daniel, therefore, got on his knees and began talking to the Lord in prayer. He began pushing their plight through in the realm of the Spirit—pushing, pushing, and pushing some more, for an entire week. He pushed like this for three weeks. After his third week of prayer and pushing in the Spirit, an angel came to his rescue. Daniel later wrote:

---

24. I strongly encourage you to read my book, *Moving in Glory Realms*, as it lays the foundation for everything I am sharing here. These concepts can be clearer and more fully understood through the revelation set forth in that book.

Then I lifted up my eyes, and looked, and behold a certain man clothed in linen, whose loins were girded with fine gold of Uphaz: his body also was like the beryl, and his face as the appearance of lightning, and his eyes as lamps of fire, and his arms and his feet like in color to polished brass, and the voice of his words like the voice of a multitude. And I Daniel alone saw the vision: for the men that were with me saw not the vision; but a great quaking fell upon them, so that they fled to hide themselves. (Daniel 10:5–7)

It is interesting that Daniel said, "*I Daniel alone saw*...." Often, when angels make their appearance, regardless of how glorious or magnificent they may seem, you might be the only one to see them. But even if you're the only one seeing an angel, don't discount what the Lord is allowing you to see. The Bible says that there were other men in the room with Daniel, but they failed to see what Daniel saw. They did, however, feel the presence of the Lord. According to the Bible, something made the other men flee. They could feel the weight of God's holiness.

When the angels of God begin to make their appearance, there is a realm of glory that comes with them. That glory realm comes to change you. When you begin interacting with angels, that heavenly realm comes upon you. It can also come upon a city, a territory, or an entire region. It comes as an impartation that others will begin to sense, discern, and pick up on. You, among others, will be changed by it.

Daniel continued:

And, behold, a hand touched me, which set me upon my knees and upon the palms of my hands. And he said unto me, O Daniel, a man greatly beloved, understand the words that I speak to you, and stand upright: for to you am I now sent. And when he had spoken this word to me, I stood trembling. (verses 10–11)

In verse 20, the angel says, "*Do you know why I have come? Soon I must return to fight against the spirit prince of the kingdom of Persia, and after that the spirit prince of the kingdom of Greece will come*" (NLT). This verse mentions three different angelic beings who represent three different nations:

Greece, Persia and Israel. Just as each nation has fallen angels who have been assigned to it, each also has holy angels who have been assigned to it.

The Angels of the Nations

God has created a group of angels who interact in the affairs of individual nations. I call these "the angels of the nations" because they watch, stand guard over, and respond to the prayers of God's people in a particular nation.

History has recorded accounts of heavenly armies assisting nations during dark times of war. During World War I, British forces were assisted by a group of angels who later came to be known as the "Angels of Mons." G. Wilson Revill, from Birmingham, England, shared:

> I was only a boy, but I well remember the anxiety in the country over the terrible battles raging in France and Belgium, with losses of men and wounded returning with unbelievable accounts of their experiences. Two soldiers, unrelated, and who did not know each other, told me and my father they saw angels hovering in the sky and the Germans retreating. The first soldier told us that most of the men in his line were either dead or wounded and there were very few of them left to fight on. They were retreating when suddenly they saw the Germans also retreating, and at that moment in the sky were angels hovering over the battlefield—he avowed it a fact.
>
> The other soldier told me that they captured a German officer who asked, "Wherever did you get your men from? We kept shooting you down but you kept on coming on at us." So it looks as if the Germans saw the angels as men, as well as our own troops seeing them.
>
> At that time, there had been, in various parts of the country, a call to prayer, and I remember the local clergyman coming to school for morning prayers, which deeply affected most of the school, for there were children there whose fathers had recently been killed, and he asked our heavenly Father "to be a husband to the widow and a father to the children"—this came from his heart.

King George V called for a National Day of Prayer when it seemed as if we had lost everything and were about to give up. So the "Angels of Mons" at that time was an answer to our prayers, and in that sense, not a mystery.[25]

Angels also help to provide direction for nations. St. Patrick, the national apostle of Ireland, had a well-known nighttime encounter with an angel known as Victoricus. In a dream, this angel delivered to him a letter entitled "The Voice of the Irish," which deeply moved him and eventually gave him the confidence to boldly spread Christianity throughout Ireland.

God has a specific purpose and call for every nation, as varied and diverse as they are in so many ways. God recognizes each of them, loves each of them, and has purposes for each of them.

My first encounter with the angels of the nations was at the Town Hall in Pukekohe, in the Auckland region of New Zealand. It was the final meeting of a month-long ministry trip, and we had invited many leaders to gather with us for a special time of intercession. As the night progressed, I saw angels gathering around the room. They were lined up, shoulder-to-shoulder, around the inside perimeter of the Town Hall auditorium.

These angels appeared to be standing at attention, ready to receive orders. I recognized them as angels of the nations, because not only were they filled with light, but because of the way they were dressed. As I have shared this revelation with others, they have told me that they were greatly encouraged because they have seen angels dressed in national outfits, or even wrapped in what appeared to be the flag of the nation they represented.

I was astonished by the presence of these angels and wondered why they were there. Sometimes, God will send such angels to alert you to a prayer need in a specific nation or to invite you on a God-ordained missionary assignment. In this case, we were praying for various nations and making declarations concerning them. I realized that these angels had come in response to our prayers, to listen to the decrees being spoken over their nations. The angels listened attentively. Then, once they had heard our declarations, they took those words back to the nations and implemented them.

---

25. "The Angels of Mons," *This England*, Winter 1982, 70.

Sometimes, when this happens, we see immediate results. At other times, it may take some time before we see any change at all. Trust God. Trust that His purposes are being fulfilled as you remain faithful to His call. God and His angels are always faithful.

At that meeting in New Zealand, we declared that impartations would be carried from the South Pole to the North Pole. As we were prophesying, some people saw in the Spirit that the Maori people of New Zealand were interacting with the Inuit people of the Canadian North. More than a decade after that meeting in New Zealand, this prophecy was fulfilled as a group of Maoris traveled north to take part in a cultural exchange in Iqaluit, Nunavut.[26]

God watches over His Word to perform it, and you can be used by God to influence nations, shift atmospheres, and change cultures, as you learn how to work with the angels of the nations.

If you're ready to start *Seeing Angels*, let's pray:

Father, I believe what Your Word teaches about angels. Just as I now recognize and welcome the ministry of angels in my personal and family life, I recognize and welcome the ministry of angels You have assigned to my church, my city, and my nation. Teach me to be more sensitive to what these angels are doing and to work with them for the accomplishment of Your purposes in each sphere of influence. In Jesus's name, and for His honor and glory, amen!

---

26. "'From one warrior nation to another': Maori take part in cultural exchange in Iqaluit," CBC, February 9, 2019, https://www.cbc.ca/news/canada/north/maori-cultural-exchange-iqaluit-1.5008751 (accessed April 24, 2019).

PART II

Recognizing Your Angels

"Make yourself familiar with the angels and behold
them frequently in spirit, for without being seen,
they are present with you."
—*St. Francis de Sales*

9

Learning to Discern Your Angels

...some have entertained angels unawares.
Hebrews 13:2

As I was finalizing the writing of this book, I made a post about angels on my social media account. Almost immediately, people began sharing their own encouraging testimonies about encountering angels in their personal lives. One lady named Georgia shared a testimony that was so exciting, I called her and asked if she could provide me with more details. Her story was about a time in her life when she was living in Temecula, California, and God sent her family an angel to help them through a difficult time of transition. Such seasons of life can stretch us, make us doubt ourselves, put holes in our bank account, and wear our patience thin. I'm so thankful that God has angels assigned to help us through such strenuous times.

I asked Georgia if I could share her testimony with you, and she agreed to let me do that. I trust that her story will bless you:

My husband and I had an encounter with an angel the year we accepted Jesus Christ into our hearts. We had lost everything twice—once in Hurricane Andrew (while living in Florida) and again after we had moved to California to "get a fresh start." Three weeks after we moved west, my husband lost his job. We had no savings, so we were desperate. After losing everything the second time, we had only one place to go, and that was directly to God. I had grown up in an atheistic family, but through a series of divine appointments, we both gave our hearts to the Lord. Now this!

For the next three Sundays, a very distinguished man approached us after the morning service. He appeared to be in his seventies, was at least six-foot-five, had short gray hair, and dressed like a cowboy.

Carrying a red Bible tucked under his arm, and with pools of love in crystal-blue eyes like I had never seen before, this "man" would gently speak to us about the absolute, unwavering love of Jesus for us. He would say, "Hold on to Jesus! Hold on!" Then he would give us a twenty-dollar bill, and that would somehow feed us and our children for the rest of that week.

Between the third and fourth Sunday, my husband's boss called and apologized for laying him off, asking if he would be willing to take his old job back. We couldn't wait to tell our new friend and to repay him for all of the kindness he had shown us. We had never asked his name. I suppose it was because the anointing was so strong on him, we simply listened to what he said without asking any questions!

After the service the next Sunday, we looked but couldn't seem to find him. We asked the pastors if they knew where he might be, but nobody seemed to know anything about the man we described. Such a large man, with cowboy boots, a big belt buckle and a tweed jacket with suede elbow patches would have been impossible to miss. But no one had any idea who we were talking about.

It was only when our pastor said, "We have never seen anyone like that here," that we knew for sure he had been an angel sent by God to help us through our difficult time of transition. God knew we would be comfortable with a cowboy, as I'm from Montana, and I met my husband in Arizona. God is so good!

Georgia and her husband had entertained an angel without even realizing it. How many angels might come across *your* path on a daily basis, and you're completely unaware of them? I don't think this is the way God wants it to be. I believe He wants us to search out the mysteries of His supernatural kingdom to become better acquainted with the realm of angels.

The great revivalist Jonathan Edwards once said, "The seeking of the kingdom of God is the chief business of the Christian life." It's God's desire for you to engage with the glory realms. I can guarantee you that He doesn't want you to be left out in the cold concerning angels, and that is why He so freely offers us the gifts of the Spirit.

As you learn to spiritually discern angels, it is important to focus your complete dependence upon the Lord Jesus Christ. He is the Great Shepherd who promises to lead us in the paths of righteousness in the glory realms. His rod, representing authority, and His staff, representing support, will bring us comfort and peace as we begin to explore these realms. All wisdom, sight, and perception must flow from our personal relationship with Jesus. He has a gift that He wants to give to each and every one of us, and that is the gift of "*discerning of spirits*" (1 Corinthians 12:10).

In the same verse, the *Amplified Bible, Classic Edition* calls this gift: "*the ability to discern and distinguish between [the utterances of true] spirits [and false ones]*" (1 Corinthians 12). By the Spirit, we can know what is holy and what is profane, what has godly motivation and what is motivated by the flesh, what is from God and what is from the enemy. This gift includes, but is not limited to, sensing the spirit realm and its beings. When discerning in this way, you will not be operating in your own natural understanding. What comes to you will come through a supernatural awareness. Discerning spirits is accomplished through the power of the Holy Spirit, as He bears witness with our spirit when something is or is not of God.

Too many people are spiritually blind, even in the church. Their eyes have been closed and their spiritual vision has been dimmed. But the Scriptures are clear: God wants us to see openly and with accurate precision—in all circumstances and situations—in order to fully manifest our God-given potential. We need to know the truth, and discerning of spirits gives us that ability.

As we have noted, whether you've been aware of it or not, angels surround your life on a daily basis. Hopefully, reading this book has given you some insight into these angels already, but having the ability to discern spirits will make you fully aware of their presence and intent—and allow you to cooperate more perfectly with them.

Not long ago, after a seminar in which I spoke about angels, many people shared their testimonies with me. One lady, Ruthann, said she had been afraid of angels all her life. Her husband would say to her, "I would love to see an angel," but her response was always, "I don't want to see an angel. That would scare me. That would terrify me. I really don't want to see an angel." But when several circumstances adversely changed in her life, she was brought to a place of crying out, "Bring them on. I need angels in my life." Within minutes of saying that, she encountered her first angel.

Too many people are blocked by fear—fear of others or fear of the unknown—blocked by their natural limited mind-set, or blocked by their natural boundaries. Some people have been blocked by their own perceptions of what they think an angel should look like or by what they've been told about how an angel should appear. The Bible clearly warns us to be careful because we may be entertaining angels unaware. (See Hebrews 13:2). This shows us that angels can either look just like us or they can come in a form that we don't immediately recognize at all. Actually, angels are able to appear in different ways to different people, depending on the different scenarios in which they are needed.

Sometimes angels are sitting, standing, or dancing among us, and we don't perceive them for who they are. Because angels are spirit beings and can present themselves in unusual ways, we need the Spirit's help to be able to discern them properly. If you would like to receive this gift of the Spirit, let's pray and ask God for it right now:

Father, I come to You in the name of Jesus. You said in Your Word that we should "eagerly desire gifts of the Spirit."[27] Therefore, I ask You for the gift of discerning spirits. Thank You for opening my heart to receive this gift from You. I believe that I receive it now,

---

27. 1 Corinthians 14:1 NIV.

so that I can perceive the spiritual atmosphere around me with clarity. In Jesus's name, amen!

In addition to this gift, we can also learn to be aware of the presence of angels by looking for clues throughout the Scriptures. In addition, I believe that God wants to give you three spiritual disciplines that will help you to cooperate with this gift of discerning spirits that has now been given to you. This will enable you to more clearly discern your angels.

Spiritual Discipline #1: Spiritual Enlightenment

The gift of discerning spirits gives you the power to see what others may not be able to see. When the disciples asked Jesus why He always spoke in parables, His answer was surprising:

> [Jesus] *replied, "Because the knowledge of the secrets of the kingdom of heaven has been given to you, but not to them."*
> (Matthew 13:11 NIV)

"*The knowledge of the secrets of the kingdom of heaven has been given to you.*" Personalize that: "The knowledge of the secrets of the kingdom has been given to *me.*" God has granted His own the privilege to see the secrets, know the secrets, and understand the secrets of His kingdom. This is a gift from God to you and me. With unbelievers, it is just the opposite:

> *The god of this age has blinded the minds of unbelievers, so that they cannot see the light of the gospel that displays the glory of Christ, who is the image of God.*   (2 Corinthians 4:4 NIV)

Satan has blinded the minds of unbelievers, and if they are to know the truth, then God must shine His light on them. It's imperative that God's light shine upon the human mind if we are to comprehend spiritual realities. We can never do it on our own. This is not something that just comes with practice. It only comes through the Spirit's gifts.

This doesn't mean that unbelievers are always oblivious to the spirit world; it just means that they can only see so far. Their vision is limited. For those who are redeemed, God provides unlimited vision into the spirit world, opening up glory realms for us to behold. Thus, we simply need to open our eyes to see and receive the spiritual beauty that God has made available for us.

Paul prayed:

*I pray that the **eyes of your heart** may be enlightened in order that you may know the hope to which he has called you, the riches of his glorious inheritance in his holy people.*   (Ephesians 1:18 NIV)

Yes, we need to be enlightened by God. This is an important key. Why don't you personalize that prayer right now and make it your own. Highlight it in your Bible and pray it over yourself for the next week. Press into this revelation, and allow God to make it personal for you:

Heavenly Father, I pray that the eyes of my heart may be enlightened in order that I may know the hope to which You have called me, the riches of Your glorious inheritance in me, Your child. In Jesus's name, amen!

Notice that Paul prayed that the *eyes of your heart* would be opened. He didn't pray for you to see clearly with the natural eyes in your head. This will be a revelation for many. You may have been praying, "God, I want to see into the spiritual dimension. I want to see angels, to see You moving, and to see the Spirit in manifestation," but this won't necessarily happen with your natural eyes. Paul prayed for the eyes of our hearts to be opened. Too many believers are looking with their natural eyes and those eyes only, but you can only see so far with your natural eyes. We need to see with the eyes of our heart. The doorway to the supernatural is through your heart, not through your head. Remember, after the angel visited Mary, the Scriptures tell us: *"Mary kept all these things, and pondered them in her heart"* (Luke 2:19). Our desire for God and His glory realm realities must flow from the heart. (See Luke 10:27.)

When the Scriptures speak of the heart, it seems clear that it actually means your spirit. So, Paul was praying for the eyes of our spirit man, our spirit eyes, to be opened. When your spirit eyes are opened, even when you are looking with your natural eyes, your spirit eyes are beginning to focus, and you can begin to see spiritual realities in the midst of anything you happen to be going through. Seeing spiritual realities requires looking with your spirit eyes—eyes of faith.

THE DOORWAY TO THE SUPERNATURAL IS THROUGH YOUR HEART, NOT THROUGH YOUR HEAD.

Some have asked me, "What does that mean? What does it mean to look with my spirit eyes?" Although my natural eyes are open, I often ask God to open my spirit eyes. I do this during worship, because I know that worship attracts heaven's presence. It is as we are praising and worshiping God that the glory begins to manifest and heavenly realities are revealed in that swirling atmosphere of heaven's sound.

When I am in worship, I know, by faith and by the Word of God, that my worship is attracting the glory. I pray, "God, I want to see with my spirit eyes what You're doing in this place." As I begin to look with my natural eyes, all the while asking God to focus my spirit eyes, I begin to see a realm transposed over this earthly realm. My spirit begins to reveal to me from within the truth of what my natural eyes are beholding from without. I begin to see a higher dimension overlaid on the earthly dimension. You can invite God's light to fill your heart this way as well.

Spiritual Discipline #2: Spiritual Clarity

Discerning spirits make things that are obscure or concealed become more obvious to the observer. The Spirit wants to remove the veil that blocks your view of the unseen spiritual dimension, so that you can see the angels who surround your life. This is what happened to the servant of Elisha:

When the servant of the man of God got up and went out early the next morning, an army with horses and chariots had surrounded the city. "Oh no, my lord! What shall we do?" the servant asked. "Don't be afraid," the prophet answered. "Those who are with us are more than those who are with them." And Elisha prayed, "Open his eyes, LORD, so that he may see." Then the LORD opened the servant's eyes, and he looked and saw the hills full of horses and chariots of fire all around Elisha. (2 Kings 6:15–17 NIV)

Seeing his servant's fearfulness of the vast army surrounding their city, Elisha prayed that God would open his eyes to see the invisible angel armies that were protecting them. The Bible says the Lord opened the eyes of the young man, and he *"saw the hills full of horses and chariots of fire all around Elisha."* Spiritual clarity will come into focus when we choose to trust God's Word and allow His Spirit to touch our sight.

Jesus prayed for a blind man:

They came to Bethsaida, and some people brought a blind man and begged Jesus to touch him. He took the blind man by the hand and led him outside the village. When he had spit on the man's eyes and put his hands on him, Jesus asked, "Do you see anything?" He looked up and said, "I see people; they look like trees walking around." Once more Jesus put his hands on the man's eyes. Then his eyes were opened, his sight was restored, and he saw everything clearly. Jesus sent him home, saying, "Don't even go into the village." (Mark 8:22–26 NIV)

Far too many believers are blind to the realities of the spirit world. The blind man of Mark 8 had his eyesight restored so that he could see everything perfectly. Is that what we all want? To see *everything?* Not just *some* things, and not just *natural* things, but to see *everything* and to see it *perfectly?* This is my prayer: "God, I want to see everything, I want 20/20 vision in the natural, and I want 20/20 vision in the spiritual."

When Jesus first touched the blind man's eyes, the man said something very interesting—that he could see people like trees walking around. I don't know about you, but I've never seen anyone as large as a tree, and I've never seen anyone who even slightly resembled a tree. Have you? Could it be that this man was seeing angels? They are often very stout and tall.

While I was conducting an Angel School in Houston, Texas, I saw an angel standing in the room. He was at least fourteen feet tall. My son, Lincoln, saw it too, and some of the students did as well. I believe that when Jesus first touched the blind man's eyes, the sight that was given to him initially was spiritual sight, and the reason he said he could see men walking as trees was because he was becoming aware of the spiritual realm and could see angels moving around. Jesus touched the man's eyes, with the desire that he see perfectly, and this included both natural and spiritual vision.

If you have been blessed with natural vision, you can see the natural things around you. Based on what you are seeing, you then make decisions about what to do and what not to do. Jesus wants to lay His hands on you and open the eyes of your heart, the eyes of your spirit, so you can say what the blind man said: "Now I see everything perfectly."

Spiritual Discipline #3: Spiritual Awareness

Discerning spirits gives us the ability to see past the natural and into supernatural realities. It allows us to become aware of spiritual truths that surround us. Paul wrote:

> So we fix our eyes not on what is seen, but on what is unseen, since what is seen is temporary, but what is unseen is eternal.
>
> (2 Corinthians 4:18 NIV)

The unseen, of course, is the spiritual. What is seen is temporary, but what is unseen is eternal. The unseen realm is the most real realm. Make that truth your own. Get this into your spirit and pray into it until you begin to wake up each morning with it on your mind. The unseen realm is the most real realm. Pray, "God, open my spirit eyes and senses, for I want to become aware of everything perfectly, so that I can know what is most real."

THE UNSEEN REALM IS THE MOST REAL REALM.

It is very possible for angels to be present and yet remain unseen in the natural, while still being felt, heard, and spiritually discerned. In the same way that God wants to open the eyes of your spirit, sometimes the way you'll begin to discern will be through your other spiritual senses, those of smelling, hearing, tasting, or touching. Often, a heavenly fragrance comes into the room when angels are beginning to move in our midst as well as when they begin to hover, an indication that they are ready for a ministry assignment.

One night, God gave a prophetic word to my spiritual mother, Dr. Billie Reagan Deck, as we were on our way together to a church service. Momma Billie told me that when she had prayed about the meeting that night, one word kept coming to her: *hover.* Sure enough, that night, angels were hovering in that place, and the presence of God was hovering there with them. Whatever anyone needed, they could just reach into the glory realm, that unseen realm, and take it.

There's a greater awareness coming to you. Draw on the truth that God is showing you in the Spirit and then just take it. For some, it might be for financial blessing. For others, it may be healing, family miracles, or emotional help. Accelerate into the promise. Receive the miracles that are coming with ease as you open your spiritual awareness to the unseen realm.

At times, when angels come into our midst, they do so carrying scrolls. These are often not for us to read but rather, to eat. When we have eaten one of these scrolls, we fully receive the revelation as we begin to taste heaven and the goodness of the Lord. Believe me, it is very sweet! The Bible says that God's Word, the revelation of Himself, is *"sweeter than honey...from the honeycomb"* (Psalm 19:10 NIV). Yes, it is very sweet.

Many times, some people see angels, while other people in the same room see nothing at all. This can be frustrating, both for the one who sees and also for the one who doesn't see. The one who sees thinks that it is all so obvious, while the one who doesn't see wonders what's wrong with them and wishes it was all so obvious. Never allow discouragement to hinder your walk of faith. It's much too precious for that.

In regard to spiritual insight, the Bible says we see in part and we prophesy in part. The *New Living Translation* renders that verse in this way:

Now our knowledge is partial and incomplete, and even the gift of prophecy reveals only part of the whole picture! (1 Corinthians 13:9)

I see a little, you see a little, and together, we have parts of the whole picture. We must learn to trust each other and cooperate with our brothers and sisters in Christ. Cooperating with the corporate vision, the overall picture that comes in the glory, is vital to our complete understanding of what God is saying and doing. Learn to appreciate the unique way in which God allows each one to tap into the glory realm.

The way you tap into this realm may be different than the way I tap into it. The way you see it may be much different than the way I see it. The things I'm aware of may be different than the things you are aware of. But when we all come together, and we each bring our individual parts of the picture—the parts we have seen, the parts we have heard, the parts we have felt, the parts we have tasted, and the parts we have smelled—it brings forth a wonderful image of the glory of God. If enough parts are joined together, it brings forth the complete vision.

Pray this prayer for God to increase your awareness of spiritual realms:

Heavenly Father, I ask for Your Spirit to open the eyes of my heart that I might become more aware. Help me discern by Your Spirit. I desire to see Your angels so that I can interact with them. I receive this gift of spiritual awareness. In Jesus's name, amen!

I would encourage you to begin exploring in God's glory. See the angels, hear the angels, and sense the angels. Cooperate with them and others to lift Jesus higher!

Both a Gift and a Discipline

Spiritual sight is both a gift to be received and a discipline to be developed. We can practice and grow in discerning spirits:

But solid food is for the mature, who by constant use have trained themselves to distinguish good from evil.　　(Hebrews 5:14 NIV)

Practice builds confidence, and repetition develops habits. This can be a good thing. Too often, we think of all habits as being bad, but godly habits are not bad at all. Spiritual habits are a necessity. Practice these disciplines that I've shared with you in this chapter. Practice your spiritual enlightenment. Practice your spiritual clarity. Practice your spiritual awareness. Then repeat the process on purpose.

I want the eyes of my heart to continually be opened. I practice this in worship and it begins to overflow into my daily walk. When I am out doing what people might call the "regular things of life," not ministering from a pulpit or laying hands on people and praying for them, but rather doing my day-to-day routine, the spiritual realm is opened for me. Why? Because I have practiced it in the Spirit, practiced it in those times of corporate praise and worship when the heavy weight of God's glory is present. Practice looking in your life, and repeat the process on purpose.

People ask me how often I see angels. The answer is that I *can* always see angels, but I *don't* always see angels. That seems like an oxymoron, doesn't it? What I mean is this: I believe that it is possible for all of us to be aware of the moving of God and His holy angels anywhere and at any time. The reason it doesn't happen is because we aren't looking. Perhaps we haven't known how to look, we haven't been paying attention, or we haven't practiced doing it enough.

I want to give you faith to understand that it is totally possible for you to come into a place of being aware of spiritual realities every day of your life, every minute of every day, and in every place you go—no matter the life circumstances.

If you're ready to start *Seeing Angels*, let's pray:

Father, I am convinced it is Your will to use angels to bless me in many ways. Help me to be alert and aware of their presence, that I might cooperate fully with them to the glory of Your name. Let Your Spirit deposit in me both the gift of discerning spirits and the willingness to develop a discipline of discerning by faithful practice. In Jesus's name, amen!

10

Meeting Your Angels

For the angel of the LORD is a guard;
he surrounds and defends all who fear him.
Psalm 34:7 (NLT)

When I was a child, seeing angels seemed normal because I and other young church friends saw them in a vivid way. We would sit together at church, on the right side of the building, and stare in amazement as the angels worshiped the Lord. Then, one day, we made the mistake of mentioning our visions to some adults in the church. Instead of being encouraged to see further into the spirit realm, we were told that it was wrong to see angels—that seeing them was actually *impossible*—and we were scolded for "lying and making things up." That was the day I stopped seeing angels because my childlike faith and sanctified imagination had been damaged.

Thank God that many years later, through the sovereignty of God, I was able to reconnect with the divine supernatural realm. Today, I am not only aware of the angels who have been assigned to *my* life, but I have been able to help others make that same connection. In a later chapter, I will share my testimony and explain how I was able to reconnect. I want to encourage you and let you know that God wants to restore your childlike faith and also your sanctified imagination. The Spirit wants to give you full awareness to engage with the angels He has created for you.

THE SPIRIT WANTS TO GIVE YOU FULL AWARENESS TO ENGAGE WITH THE ANGELS HE HAS CREATED FOR YOU.

Childlike Faith Restored

Speaking about faith, Jesus said: *"Truly I tell you, unless you change and become like little children, you will never enter the kingdom of heaven"* (Matthew 18:3 NIV). If we want to enter into these supernatural heavenly realities, we must return to a childlike faith. Many people feel as though their childlike faith has been lost because of life experiences in their past, perhaps due to trauma, abuse, and any number of other reasons. I believe God both wants to and has the ability to restore your faith like that of a child.

I want to examine this specific kind of faith for a moment. I have created an acronym using the word CADET to best describe the individual elements of childlike faith. According to the dictionary, the archaic meaning for the word *cadet* is "a younger son or daughter." It also means "a trainee." Now, let's examine the meaning of my acronym, CADET.

C	Confident
A	Awe-inspired
D	Discovering
E	Expectant
T	Tenacious

Confident

Childlike faith is confident in the input, instructions, and guidance of an older mentor. It does not waver at all, but completely trusts the advice and knowledge provided. It fully believes what has been spoken and promised. *"Being confident of this very thing, that He which has begun a good work in you will perform it until the day of Jesus Christ"* (Philippians 1:6). Regarding angels, we must discover what the Scriptures say (which we are doing in this book) and have complete confidence in the final authority of God's Word, regardless of what others may say or how others respond to this revelation.

Awe-inspired

The dictionary defines the word *awe* as "a feeling of reverential respect mixed with fear or wonder." *Wonder* is defined as "a feeling of amazement and admiration, caused by something beautiful, remarkable, or unfamiliar." This could also be "a surprising event or situation," as in "an awe-struck moment." Childlike faith is full of awe and wonder. The Bible shows us that God is awesome! As you prepare to encounter your angels, get ready for moments of surprise and overwhelming beauty. Jacob saw angels ascending and descending upon a ladder in his dream, and his response was: *"How awesome is this place! This is none other than the house of God; this is the gate of heaven"* (Genesis 28:17 NIV). God wants you to be awed too.

Discovering

God gives us permission to explore. Of course, this must always be done under the protection of the blood of Jesus and within the spiritual safety of His Word. Childlike faith is filled with curiosity and discovery.

Have you ever noticed that little children love to ask questions? There is so much for them to discover! *"But if from there you shall seek the LORD your God you shall find Him, if you seek Him with all your heart and with all your soul"* (Deuteronomy 4:29). There is always more to learn, see, hear, touch, taste, and smell, and you will discover in this book that even your natural senses can be activated spiritually to discern. Discovery breeds creativity and sparks the imagination. Throughout the Gospels, we see Jesus speaking in parables, entertaining the minds of those who were listening and captivating the imaginations of the masses. The Spirit wants to anoint your mind to discover more spiritual dimensions with Jesus through a sanctified imagination.

One of my favorite things to do is to find Scriptures and subjects in the Bible that open up new doorways into the Spirit. This has led me on some great adventures with God. I believe He wants you to discover new realms in Him too!

Expectant

Have you ever noticed that children are always expectant? They want to know when the next thing will happen, what they will be eating next, when they will get to play with their friends, when they will arrive at their destination, etc. There is so much expectancy in childhood! As God restores our childlike faith, we should have that same expectation for the things He wants to do in our lives! We've received this instruction through the Scriptures: *"If you believe, you will receive whatever you ask for in prayer"* (Matthew 21:22 NIV). We should expect angel encounters, we should expect to hear angels and see angels, we should expect to receive everything that God has said we can have, according to His Word, and that includes angel encounters.

Tenacious

Childlike faith is a tenacious faith! It will not relent! It will not give up! It will continue to seek, pursue, and persist until it obtains the promise. As young children, we were always like this; so what happened to us as adults? The Bible says: *"Ask, and it shall be given you; seek, and you shall find; knock, and it shall be opened to you"* (Matthew 7:7). Be tenacious for the things of God.

The Spirit will train us and open divine connections for us, as we allow Him to restore our childlike faith and help us to become a CADET believer. Our childlike faith aligns us to receive the insight and obtain our spiritual promises as we move forward. I want to encourage you to take some time and pray into the individual elements of this acronym. If you want to meet your angels, you will need to be a confident, awe-inspired, discovering, expectant, and tenacious believer! Can you do that?

A Sanctified Imagination

These days, when I mention the word *imagination*, it is frowned on by most Christian believers. They assume that I'm talking about having a thought that does not correspond to the reality of things in the "real world." But your imagination is simply the inner operations of your mind. It is the part of you that connects with the unseen world, but that world is very real indeed. Just because it is unseen to your natural eyes doesn't mean that it doesn't exist. There are many things that we cannot see with our eyes; this is why God has given us an imagination, the part of us that is able to see beyond mere earthly realities.

Consider this: everything that has ever been created was first imagined. Your imagination is God's gift to you, and in the Scriptures, we are instructed to have the mind of Christ. (See Philippians 2:5.) When Jesus walked the earth, do you believe He was able to see more than what was naturally presented before Him? I do. I personally believe that was why He was able to walk on water, pass through walls, perform miracles, prophesy with accuracy, know the hearts of men, and, ultimately, journey to the cross of Calvary. Think about this for a moment. If Jesus didn't know how to use His imagination in a sanctified way, why would He have put mud in the blind man's eyes? I believe that Jesus imagined that mud being used as a substance, much in the same way that God created man from the dust of the earth, and in Jesus's mind, He could see it being formed into eyeballs. From this vision in His mind, Jesus spoke out divine instructions, and, of course, the rest is history. The man was perfectly healed! (See John 9:1–7.)

The Bible declares this about Jesus: "*...who for the joy that was set before Him endured the cross, despising the shame*" (Hebrews 12:2). The joy that was set before Jesus had to be a vision, or picture, that He could see in His imagination. It certainly wasn't a natural vision of the agony and terror that He would face.

Jesus spoke in parables to the people of His day, and we can find twenty-four of those parables recorded in the Scriptures. It was Jesus's imagination that allowed Him to connect to the very heart of the Father. And, in turn, it was through His imagination that He was able to connect others to the heart of the Father.

The word *imagination* carries the following definition: "The faculty of forming new ideas, or of images or concepts of external objects not present to the senses." In other words, although you may not be able to naturally see, smell, hear, taste, or touch something, your imagination will allow you to form an understanding of what can only be spiritually perceived.

Many in the church have been afraid of this realm because of the words of 2 Corinthians 10:5, which speaks of *"casting down [vain] imaginations."* Let's look at that Scripture for a moment to see what it's really speaking about:

Casting down imaginations, and every high thing that exalts itself against the knowledge of God, and bringing into captivity every thought to the obedience of Christ.

This is a powerful instruction, encouraging us to cast down *"every high thing that exalts itself against the knowledge of God."* Our imaginations must be consecrated and brought into submission to God and His ways. If the apostle Paul felt strongly enough to address this issue, it must have been because he understood the power of our imagination. He knew that God desires to speak to us and exalt Himself through that process. After all, the Bible also says: *"For as [a man] thinks in his heart, so is he"* (Proverbs 23:7). We must cast down vain imaginations, bringing them into the obedience of Christ, so that He might sanctify our imagination for His glory.

Let's pray for God to do this in our life:

Father, I humble myself before You. I ask You to consecrate my heart and my mind with the purity and holiness of Your light. Come and sanctify my imagination for Your glory. I command all vain imaginations to be cast down, and ask that the thoughts, ideas, and flow of creativity in my spirit would come into obedience to Your Word and Your Spirit. I ask for Your Holy Spirit to cover and protect me, as You lead me into all truth. In Jesus's cleansing name, amen!

If you have been dealing with night terrors, or a wandering mind, you may want to write out this prayer and speak it over yourself at night before you lay down to rest and every morning when you wake up.

Three Biblical Ways Our Angels Appear

As we position ourselves to receive more of God's light and life by setting our minds on heavenly things (see Colossians 3:2), we can expect our angels to show up and make themselves known to us. There are many different ways in which God allows you to meet your angels—and I believe that He *does* want you to meet them. He created them to serve you!

Although, in reality, there are unlimited means through which angels can make themselves known to you, we see them appearing to people predominantly in one of three ways within the pages of the Bible.

1. Angels Appear in Physical Form

When this happens, it is often not recognized as an angel encounter at the time—unless, of course, you learn to discern the signs of their presence. This is why the Bible instructs us: *"Be not forgetful to entertain strangers: for thereby some have entertained angels unawares"* (Hebrews 13:2). Abraham met three angels who appeared to be human visitors. (See Genesis 18:1–15.) Lot showed hospitality to two angels who appeared to be mere strangers. (See Genesis 19:1–3.)

When you meet angels in this way, you will generally not recognize them as angels at first, but they have been sent by God on a special mission. Some of my friends have told me stories about angels who helped to lead them (and carry their bags!) through a foreign airport, assisted with changing a flat tire on the side of a busy road, or paid for groceries when they had run out of money. In my own life, I can testify about "ordinary angels" showing up at different times to do ordinary things.

It seems to me that angels often appear cloaked as humans when they need to work with you in a practical way or accomplish a clear objective. Not long ago, I asked the Lord about this. "God," I asked, "why don't You allow us to recognize Your angels immediately when they come to us in a physical appearance as humans?" In my spirit, I felt Him respond, "Joshua, on most occasions, that would distract from the purpose for which I sent them. However, if it brings peace and comfort to My children, I will allow them to be recognized."

For this reason, I believe God allows angels to come most times as strangers in our midst, to serve His purposes, without giving any room for interruption. Normally, it's not until after angels have left our company that we even realize we've been in the presence of an angel.

2. Angels Appear in Visions

Often, we speak about dreams and visions in the same breath, but there is a distinct difference between the two. Visions are unlike dreams in that they take place when an individual is awake, and the only person who can see the angel is the one having the vision. Ezekiel had several encounters with cherubim in this way (see Ezekiel chapters 1 and 10), and John had fifty-two angelic encounters that are recorded in the book of Revelation.

In his book, *Visions Beyond the Veil*, American missionary H. A. Baker wrote about the supernatural experiences that children were having at the Adullam Orphanage in Yunnan Province in China:

> ...many of the children saw angels near or in the room. When they were hindered by demonic power they saw angels come to their release. On occasions of the most blessed sense of the presence of the Lord in our midst and of the sweetest harmony and love in the meeting, just above the room was a large angel, while the room was entirely surrounded by smaller angels standing side by side, each touching the other to the right and left, so there was not a space in the whole circle for the entrance of any demon.[28]

Many times in our meetings, I will be aware of angels in the room through what I call an open-eye vision. Some people receive visions in their spirit, which are much more like impressions, or "knowings," that something is occurring in the atmosphere. Either of these methods is legitimate.

3. Angels Appear in Dreams

Joseph, the husband of Mary, had several dreams in which an angel came to give him both an instruction (see Matthew 1:20–21) and a warning (see Matthew 2:13). The first visitation came so that Joseph could fully

---

28. H. A. Baker, *Visions Beyond the Veil* (New Kensington, PA: Whitaker House, 1973, 2006), 97.

understand what his role would be if he took Mary as his wife. The second visitation was to make sure he understood that he needed to take his new family and flee to Egypt in order to protect Jesus's life.

As noted, Jacob had a dream in which he saw angels ascending and descending on a heavenly ladder. (See Genesis 28:12.) When he awoke, he recognized that the dream had been a valid God-encounter, so much so that he dedicated the stone that he had used as a pillow and proclaimed that location as *the gate of heaven* (Genesis 28:17).

For me personally, it was through the dream realm that I was reconnected with my guardian angels after so many years of spiritual dormancy. God has a way for you to connect with your angels too. Trust Him and allow Him to lead you as you receive the revelation in this book.

Whether an angel appears in person through a vision or in a dream doesn't make the experience any more or any less supernatural. The angel Gabriel suddenly appearing to Mary in a visible way (see Luke 1:26–38) was no more miraculous than Joseph's nighttime dream, in which he saw an angel (see Matthew 1:20–21). The method God chooses is always valid and we must learn to appreciate the various ways in which angels can make their introductions to us.

Some people are so determined to see an angel with their eyes wide open that they resist the simple ease of seeing angels through the eyes of their spirit. I am teaching you how to become more receptive to the various ways in which angels appear.

Angels Among Us

There have been several times in my life when I knew without a doubt that I had met an angel, one that initially appeared to be just a stranger. These angels have sometimes come as help in an airport, as an escort through rush-hour traffic, as an informative "person" on the side of the road, or in other ways. I'm not talking about a regular person who seems to be helpful, and so we say, "Oh, that person is such an angel." No! I'm speaking about actual heaven-sent angels, assigned to walk among us mysteriously disguised as everyday people. I'm sure that not until we reach heaven will we learn of all the times in which we've been surrounded by angels and didn't realize it.

I want you to use the chart on the next page to record some past angel experiences you've had and to record future encounters as they come. This chart will help you to keep track of these special moments when God sends His angels to minister to you.

In his book, *Angels to Help You*, Lester Sumrall shared a story about an angel coming to his home when he was a young boy:

> ...a stranger once came to our door and asked to be fed. My mother agreed, provided the meal, and then sensed something unusual about him. Right after he left she opened the door, but he was nowhere in sight. Mother became aware that she may have been entertaining an angel.[29]

Sometimes, angels come simply to watch and record your responses; at other times, they come to help you through a difficult situation or to enable you to minister much more effectively to others.

Several years ago, a friend and I were visiting Hollywood. As we were walking down Hollywood Boulevard, we noticed some activity being filmed on the sidewalk in front of us. We didn't recognize the celebrities who were involved, but we continued to watch as they played music and created quite a bit of excitement for the crowd that gathered. Then, a lady approached us from behind and asked if we would like to know more about what was going on. We were delighted that she could help fill us in, not just on *what* was happening but also *who* we were watching.

She started by telling us the name of one of the actors involved, also stating that he was an enormously popular musical star overseas. She told us private details of his home life and some personal difficulties that seemed to be troubling him. All of this seemed like too much information, and I remember thinking, *Wow, if this lady is as close to this man as it seems, she really shouldn't be telling this information to strangers on the street.* When I turned to ask the woman another question, she was gone. We wondered,

---

29. Lester Sumrall, *Angels to Help You* (New Kensington, PA: Whitaker House, 1982), 88.

Angels Among Us Tracking Sheet

Date	Place	Briefly describe details of the encounter.	How did it make you feel? What were the results?

"Just as the mountains surround Jerusalem, so the LORD surrounds his people, both now and forever."   (Psalm 125:2 NLT)

Where did she go? She hadn't even said goodbye. I quickly dismissed her disappearance.

Later that day, my friend and I decided to eat at a steakhouse in Beverly Hills. We were the first ones seated at dinner time, but, believe it or not, about twenty minutes later, the celebrity we had seen earlier on the street was seated at the very next table. Because we knew so much about him, we also knew how to pray for him. It was a divine set-up! We were able to lay our hands on the man and speak blessings over him, as well as take a photo of this special moment.

Later, when we had time to think about it, we came to the conclusion that the woman we encountered on Hollywood Boulevard who told us all of those things had actually been an angel. She had appeared in the form of a normal person, but she gave us strategies and told us details that enabled us to be more effective in our prayers for that young man.

About a year later while I was ministering in South Korea, I saw that same man giving an interview on television. He was sharing his testimony about how the Lord had saved him and led him to begin one of the largest youth ministries in Asia. Praise the Lord! That's how angels work.

Meeting My Guardian Angels

As I noted before, I first met some of my angels when I was just a young child. Unfortunately, I was not able to grow in supernatural insight about angels because this realm was closed to me due to the negative words spoken by an adult, who, I'm sure, was only trying to do the right and rational thing. Almost twenty years passed before this glorious realm was reopened to me.

It happened at Calvary Campground in Ashland, Virginia, and it happened through a dream. One night after the campmeeting service, I went to sleep, and in the middle of the night, I had a dream in which three different angels appeared to me and introduced themselves as angels who were assigned over my life. These large angels were wearing brilliant robes and they glowed with a golden luster, just like the angels I had seen as a child. The thing that struck me about all three of them, however, was their appearance: they resembled me!

These angels were much taller and broader than I was and each one of them had a distinctive hairstyle and eye color. Still, they looked just like my angelic brothers.

When I asked them their names, each one responded, saying they were Caramat, Zimri, and Ryan, in that order. I asked why God had allowed me to see them, and they began to describe their ministry functions and assignments. They had been assigned as special guardians in my life.

The first angel, Caramat, was assigned to bring creative miracles, signs, and wonders. That is part of my assignment on earth, to release the message of God's glory, and when I do, this angel accompanies me, working for God as a ministering angel, to me and to those I minister to. Interestingly enough, since that time, many people have told me they see a "golden angel" standing behind me when I preach. I know this is Caramat because he has been assigned to me and he travels with me everywhere I go, whether I see him or not.

The second angel, Zimri, told me that he had been assigned to bring forth the new song. Imagine that! There are angels who bring new songs from heaven. Sometimes, Zimri will feed my spirit notes and scrolls while I'm singing, and this will cause the song of the Lord to come forth.

The third angel, Ryan, told me that he was assigned to bring me holy boldness and strength. There have been times when I have physically felt him show up. There have also been times when timidity was trying to make me weak in the knees about what I was to do. God wanted me to say something and I wasn't sure whether I could say it or not. I didn't want to offend anyone. But there are times when God will have me say something very direct and with great boldness, and that is never easy for me. That's when Ryan shows up, and such boldness comes upon me that I say things that surprise even me.

Was this just another dream I had? It seemed extremely vivid and real to me. I believe it was a heavenly encounter. What I can say for sure is that a whole new realm was suddenly opened to me, and I felt aware of my angels after that. I'm so thankful that the Spirit allowed me to again access this dimension after many years of dormancy in my spiritual walk. From that time, the presence of angels has continued to increase in my life and ministry.

After that experience, I began to research, pursue, and posture myself for further revelation regarding these amazing heavenly messengers. And God can use your dreams to open the realm of angels for you too.

If you're ready to start *Seeing Angels*, let's pray:

Lord, I believe in You, I am assured of heaven, and I trust in the ministry work of Your angels. Thank You for restoring my child-like faith—faith that simply believes what my heart receives from You. Thank You for speaking to me through Your Word and through this book about the authenticity of Your angels in my life. I boldly ask You for eye-opening encounters, visions, and dreams that will confirm what Your Word has already spoken to me in this regard. In Jesus's name, amen!

11

Your Angels Have a Name

Surely goodness and mercy shall follow me all the days of my life:
and I will dwell in the house of the LORD for ever.
Psalm 23:6

Here, David referred to his angels by name, calling them "Goodness" and "Mercy." Had you ever noticed that before? David wasn't just speaking about the attributes of God here; he was speaking about two guardian angels who he knew had been assigned to his life.

This is why we pray for "traveling mercies." When we pray for someone who is going on a trip, and we ask God to give them "traveling mercies," we're literally asking Him to assign specific angels to go with them, to guard them on their journey. Often, we have prayed, "Lord, let Your angels go ahead and behind, above and below, to the left and the right, as we travel in Your light." These angels will have a name.

In *The Treasury of David Commentary*, Charles H. Spurgeon explained:

These twin guardian angels will always be with me at my back and my beck. Just as when great princes go abroad they must not go unattended, so it is with the believer. Goodness and mercy follow him always—all the days of his life—the black days as well as the bright days, the days of fasting as well as the days of feasting, the dreary days of winter as well as the bright days of summer. Goodness supplies our needs, and mercy blots out our sins.[30]

From a slightly different perspective, author Max Lucado writes, "If the Lord is the shepherd who leads the flock, goodness and mercy are the two sheepdogs that guard the rear of the flock."[31] I like both of these explanations, because they give us confidence, knowing that God assigned His angels over David's life for a specific purpose, and that God has angels assigned over our lives too! And, again, they have names.

Angels Reveal Their Names in a Dream

As I mentioned in the last chapter, many years ago, I had a dream while sleeping over the snack bar at Calvary Campground in Ashland, Virginia. In that dream, I was lifted into an ethereal sphere above the earth, where I encountered three of my guardian angels. These angels introduced themselves to me by name and began explaining their purpose and ministry functions in my life. Lincoln was very small at the time, just a toddler, and he had been talking a lot about someone named Dana. We could never figure out who he was talking about because we didn't have any family or friends by that name. Well, we didn't understand it until the night when I met my angels in a dream. In that dream, I also met Janet's angels and Lincoln's angels.

When Lincoln's head angel introduced himself to me as Dana, whoa, was I ever surprised! All that time, Lincoln had been talking about an angel, and we had been totally unaware of its presence.

After this encounter, we began to do our research and discovered that Dana is a Hebrew name that means "God Is Judge." This was extremely significant to us as a family, because we were young and new to the ministry; and yet, God was doing profound (some would say "controversial")

---

30. Charles Spurgeon, *The Treasury of David*, Bible Study Tools, https://www.biblestudytools.com/commentaries/treasury-of-david/psalms-23-6.html (accessed May 13, 2019).

31. Max Lucado, "God's Sheepdogs: Goodness and Mercy," FaithGateway.com, June 26, 2013, https://www.faithgateway.com/gods-sheepdogs-goodness-and-mercy/#.XNnkbXx7m71 (accessed May 13, 2019).

supernatural things in our lives. We had begun experiencing many unusual signs, wonders, and miracles, which seemed to bring us much persecution everywhere we went. We were often misunderstood and wrongly accused. What an encouragement to know that God had placed His angel, Dana, in the center of our lives! God Is Judge! It reminded us that God has the final word, and it gave us the confidence to move forward in the ministry assignment set before us.

Angels Named Joy and Abundance

Sometimes, when people ask their angels about their names, the name and its meaning are obvious. Recently, while I was in Taipei, Taiwan, I was teaching the people how to connect with their angels. One lady asked her angel about his name, and he responded by saying that his name was Joy. She was thrilled and almost immediately began breaking out in laughter. The atmosphere became charged by the presence of God released through that encounter, and soon, the entire room erupted with sounds of ecstatic joy. It was obvious to us that the angel named Joy had come to minister to us. However, this angel came to bring us closer to Jesus, as He is our focus.

That same lady also discovered that she had another angel named Abundance. That same day, she received an unexpected financial blessing in her personal business, three times the amount she would normally have earned in a week's time. Joy and Abundance had not only introduced themselves to her by name, but they also demonstrated their function in her life in tangible ways. She just needed to learn how to cooperate with them.

We will speak about working with your angels in part three of this book, but the first step is learning how to make the initial introduction. Offering someone your name is the very first step toward developing a relationship with them. This is the way we introduce ourselves to others, and we should expect our angels to do the same when they are introducing themselves to us. What you'll discover about your angels is that when you meet them, they will never bring glory to themselves. Their names carry a ministry assignment from God, and this, in itself, should direct your attention back to Him.

What Is Your Angel's Name?

"I am Gabriel. I stand in the presence of God, and I have been sent to speak to you." (Luke 1:19 NIV)

Scripturally, you can ask your angel about its name, and I think you should. When Manoah inquired of the angel who visited him about his name, he responded by telling Manoah it was Wonderful. (See Judges 13:17–18.) Angels with descriptive names like Healing, Deliverance, Charisma, Harvest, Voice, or Glory are obvious in their assignments to deliver what their name implies. But sometimes the name and meaning don't seem so obvious and require a bit of research and inquiring of the Holy Spirit to understand.

When Pastor Rolland Buck encountered his angels, they introduced themselves as Gabriel and Chrioni. He later learned that Gabriel was the same angel of ancient times who had appeared to saints in the Bible, while Chrioni was a warrior angel.

As noted earlier in the book, when my friend Patricia King had a vision of the angel who was assigned to her ministry, she came to know that his name was Swift, and she quickly learned that he had been assigned for prophetic acceleration.

When I had the dream in which I met my three guardian angels, they introduced themselves as Caramat, Zimri, and Ryan, each carrying their own ministry assignment in my life—delivering miracles, new songs, and boldness and strength.

"Ask, and You Shall Receive"

Ask, and it shall be given you; seek, and you shall find; knock, and it shall be opened to you. (Matthew 7:7)

What is your angel's name? Every angel sent by God is called to a specific function, but the first task is to inquire about their name. You may want to do this during a quiet time of prayer and devotion, as you're waking up in the morning, or even as you're lying down to sleep at night. The main thing is not to feel rushed or forced. Spiritual things come to us more easily when we position ourselves to open up to God in an atmosphere of rest. I have an album called *Activating Angels in Your Life* that I think you would be able to assist you in coming into these things more easily. It is a great companion resource to this book and includes a track called "Meeting Your Guardian Angel," which will help you do just that!

Several weeks ago, after I had finished a session in Santa Barbara, California, a young man approached me at the book table. He told me that he had followed my instructions and felt that his angel's name was Greg. Now that might seem too ordinary for some people, or too common a name. I asked him, "Did you look it up, to find out what it means?"

He replied with an enthusiastic, "Yes! It means 'Watchful and Alert'!"

"That's wonderful!" I told him. "God has revealed to you that you have a watcher angel assigned to your life. Daniel also had some experiences with watchers." (See Daniel 4:13–17.) The young man was encouraged to know the name of his angel and felt more confident about going forward with the call of God on his life.

An Angel Named Bob

There was a lady in Ireland who asked her angel for his name, and he responded by saying that his name was Bob. The name Bob might not sound spiritual at all, but remember that it is derived from Robert and, upon careful research, you will discover that Robert means "Bright and Shining." Wow! Could it be that Bob is a seraph, shining with God's fire and brilliance?

Once you ask your angel for its name, listen carefully, and then prayerfully consider the name you receive. You might need to do some research and ask some other trusted friends for their input, but the answer will probably amaze you!

Knowing the name of your angel can help to reveal something important in regard to their characteristics, function, and main purpose in your life. Remember, they are sent to serve you. (See Hebrews 1:14.) We partner with angels for God's purposes. We never worship them or pray to them, but we certainly appreciate them, we thank God for them, and, like the psalmist David, we have peace, knowing that these heavenly beings are following us everywhere we go, as we choose to live in the presence of God.

If you're ready to start *Seeing Angels*, let's pray:

Heavenly Father, I choose to give You glory today! My heart is filled with gratitude for all that You have done and all that You have provided for me. Thank You for assigning specific angels to my life who will enable me to fulfill Your call. Help me to be more aware of this spiritual realm. Help my ears to hear and my spirit to perceive the name, assignment, and purpose of the heavenly messengers You have sent to me, so that I can cooperate with them fully in serving You! In the name of Jesus, amen!

12

Angel Communications and Our Response

The people therefore, that stood by, and heard it, said that it thundered: others said, An angel spoke to Him. Jesus answered and said, This voice came not because of Me, but for your sakes.
John 12:29–30

Have you ever sensed that your angels were trying to communicate with you? Have you felt their presence surrounding you and somehow knew that God had sent them with a special message? I've noticed that most angel communications happen during the late-night or early-morning hours, and that there are specific seasons of the year in which these spiritual lines of connection seem to be more open than at other times.

As I travel around the world, I often hear testimonies from people who have sensed their angels attempting to reach out to them, but more often than not, they haven't understood how to properly respond. This can be frustrating.

In this chapter, I want to share some of my personal experiences and some angel encounters in the Bible that will help you understand the ways angels communicate and the various ways in which we should rightly respond to the messages they bring.

If you want to begin *Seeing Angels*, one of the best things you can do is let go of your preconceived ideas about the way you think they *should* appear. Angels can present themselves in many different ways, and we must be open to "see" them in whatever form God chooses to send them to us—whether through sight, sound, feeling, or any other way to spiritually sense their presence. We don't get to choose how they come but we do get to choose how we receive their communications. This is much like the way we choose to tune into a radio signal. We must be willing to tune the dial to receive the signal!

How Angels Communicate

Sometimes, when angels want to bring us a message, they use their voices (we will discuss this later in the chapter), but generally speaking, the messages angels bring come to us in other ways, ways that must be recognized.

The first thing you need to understand is that all spiritual communication can be classified under one of two headings: subtle communications or overt communications. Subtle communications are delicate and faint, and they require both mental acuteness and spiritual discernment in order to perceive that your angels are attempting to reach out to you. Overt communications are plain and apparent, but they must also be discerned spiritually. Here are seven scriptural ways angels communicate with us:

1. A Knowing

There are times when I have experienced a sudden awareness in my spirit, a "knowing" that God's angels are surrounding me. In those times, it's as though I can feel that somebody is watching me. (I'm not speaking about paranoia here; I'm talking about the inward witness of my spirit becoming aware of the presence of angels around me.)

We already know, by the Word of God, that He has assigned guardian angels to watch over us continually. Those angels never leave our side. But there are times when you will suddenly become aware of them, sensing their protection, and knowing that you are being kept safe from potential harm. This is subtle communication. When communicating with angels in this way, you will not be operating in your natural understanding; it will be through a supernatural knowing.

In chapter eight, we discussed the gift of discerning spirits, and we know that this is accomplished through the power of the Holy Spirit, who bears witness with our spirit when something is or is not of God. For instance, we see that Peter discerned Cornelius' angel encounter in this way:

> Cornelius answered: "Three days ago I was in my house praying at this hour, at three in the afternoon. Suddenly a man in shining clothes stood before me and said, 'Cornelius, God has heard your prayer and remembered your gifts to the poor. Send to Joppa for Simon who is called Peter. He is a guest in the home of Simon the tanner, who lives by the sea.' So I sent for you immediately, and it was good of you to come. Now we are all here in the presence of God to listen to everything the Lord has commanded you to tell us." Then Peter began to speak: "I now realize how true it is that God does not show favoritism but accepts from every nation the one who fears him and does what is right."
>
> (Acts 10:30–35 NIV)

The language of angels is a heavenly one. Messages that come to us in a spiritual way are undiluted; they shine light and life into our situations. When Jesus spoke on the earth, He said that His words were *"spirit, and... life"* (John 6:63). When God chooses to deliver a message to us through His angels, it will also come with spirit and life, simply because it is His message. The beauty in this type of communication is that it is perfect, pure, and prevents any misunderstanding.

This is what the Bible speaks about when it says that in heaven, we *"shall know fully, even as [we are] fully known"* (1 Corinthians 13:12 NIV). As you learn to trust the spirit flow of thoughts that come to you in this way, you will gain confidence in implementing any new ideas, suggestions, or changes that angels communicate to you.

2. Atmosphere

I mentioned that your guardian angels never leave your side, but some ministering spirits do. The job of ministering spirits is to retrieve blessings, impartations, and gifts from heaven and bring them to earth to bless your life. An example of this would be Jacob's dream in Genesis 28, in which he witnessed angels ascending to heaven on a ladder and then descending back to earth. As a result, the atmosphere changed and Jacob declared his location an opening to heaven.

When these ministering spirits begin to move, we can often feel their movements in the atmosphere around us—if we're willing to discern their subtle communication. Sometimes, I can feel a vibration in the atmosphere, and it will even reverberate in my chest. That's always an indicator to me that angels are hovering nearby.

The Bible calls these angels *"winds"* and *"flames of fire"* (Psalm 104:4 NLT). Often, angels will even bring a temperature change to the atmosphere. You may feel a warming or a cooling breeze, as the movement of angel wings creates a flurry of air on your hands or face during worship. (See Hebrews 1:7.) I have experienced this phenomenon on several occasions.

Once, while working on a music album in a recording studio, I became so caught up in worship that it seemed as if I was physically in heaven. During this experience, I felt the feathers of angel wings brushing across my face with such vibrant and energetic force that the intensity felt like the rotating brushes of a carwash. This experience continued for several minutes and all I could do was respond by singing in heavenly tongues, which I believe is the language of angels. (See 1 Corinthians 13:1.)

This was an invigorating and refreshing encounter with my heavenly messengers, and the message that came to me in those moments was that God would use my music to release purity in the places where it was played. In fact, we have received testimonies of that very thing happening. Become aware of the presence of angels in the atmosphere around you.

3. Signs and Wonders

In Romans 15:19, Paul states that the full gospel of Jesus Christ is preached when it is accompanied by *"mighty signs and wonders."* Signs and wonders draw people to Christ. They are visible demonstrations of the reality of God's miraculous power working in the earth. But have you ever stopped to think about how God chooses to release these signs and wonders?

The Bible is clear that God will do it through the lives of willing believers who trust His Word and boldly activate it. But just as the Lord has provided angels in your life for other needs, I am assured that God has also provided angels to assist in the release of signs and wonders over the earth.

When I initially met three of my angels in that dream, the first one introduced himself to me by name and told me that he had been assigned to bring miraculous signs into the earth through my life and ministry. When we witness the diverse visible manifestations being revealed in our meetings, they always point us to Jesus, but I am also aware that they are often delivered by angels. There are manifestations that occur more often when angels are involved, including heavenly fragrances, the appearance of feathers, and creative miracles. When you receive a thought or feeling, or become suddenly aware of these signs more than twice during a short period of time, that is often a confirmation to you that God is speaking clearly, and that His angels are trying to alert you of His presence.

I've often said: "When God speaks once, you'd better listen, but when God speaks twice, you'd better get ready!" When you begin to witness signs and wonders in your life, you can be sure that God is sending you a message through His angels. (I will address this again in chapter 13.)

4. Dreams

We already discussed initial encounters and meeting your angels in dreams, but there are also times when angels may appear in your dreams to deliver a solution to a specific problem you are facing or to bring advice concerning something that has been bothering you. By morning, you will notice that you feel much more positive because you have a clear direction of the right path to take and the proper decisions to make.

Jacob received wisdom from angels through a dream (see Genesis 31:10–12), likewise, we need to be careful not to disregard the supernatural encounters the Lord enables us to witness through the dream realm. The Lord uses our dreams to deliver messages and wisdom through His angels. (See Matthew 1:20, 2:12–13, 19).

Pay close attention to the numbers or patterns you receive, along with the specific colors you notice as they often carry prophetic wisdom and timely messages needing to be decoded. It would be wise to keep a pen and dream journal on your bed stand to carefully document these encounters while they are still fresh in your spirit.

5. *Visions*

Angels appeared to Mary to inform her that she was chosen, among all women, to give birth to the Messiah. (See Luke 1:26–28.) They announced the birth of Jesus to shepherds outside of Bethlehem. (See Luke 2:9–14.) Peter was rescued from jail by the visitation of an angel through a vision. (See Acts 12:6–10.) Paul received his calling through a prophetic revelation from an angel. (See Acts 27:21–25.)

Joan of Arc spoke about seeing the biblical angel, Michael, as well as other heavenly hosts who would often appear to her. She said, "I saw them with my bodily eyes, as clearly as I see you; and when they departed I used to weep, and wish that they would take me with them."[32] History records that these angelic encounters ultimately helped her to lead the French army to victory at the tender age of seventeen.

The Bible cautions us that angels can appear so frequently that we may even think they are merely strangers. These visions of angels are overt, but at other times, angels can visibly appear much more subtly as flashing light (see Luke 2:9), orbs of light (see James 1:17), beings clothed in cloud formations (see Daniel 7:13; Psalm 104:3), or as shadows (see Psalm 63:7).

Angela Pinkston, a worship leader from Albany, Oregon, told me:

I have a big angel that stands behind me when I lead worship. People from all over the world who don't know each other will find me after a time of worship and tell me about this huge angel they have seen! It makes me smile every time!

Kirstie shared her experience with an angel:

I saw a blue, almost transparent, angel a foot taller than my pastor, and he was standing directly behind him. It was as if the angel

---

32. Andrew Lang, *The Maid of France: Being the Story of the Life and Death of Jeanne D'Arc* (London: Longmans, Green and Co.) 1908), 44.

was there to protect the message my pastor was delivering to the church.

It is very common for me to see angels in silhouette form. Initially, I am only able to recognize their outline and not the defining details of their being. Don't worry if you only see partial aspects of an angel. You are only responsible to see what God is revealing to you. When you have begun to see in part, prophesy and speak out what you're seeing. I've discovered that if I pray and prophesy into what I'm seeing, which takes an amount of faith, the Lord will allow my spirit to glean more details.

About a decade ago, I was listening to Scriptures and working at my computer late one night and I looked up to see a parade of angels walking into my bedroom. I could see their frame, like an aura around their heads, necks, and shoulders, but I could not clearly see their faces or their bodies. By spiritual perception, I knew that these angels commonly walked through my house.

A few nights later, I saw the angels again. I was watching a televised teaching about the healing power of God. This time, the Holy Spirit revealed to me that these were angels assigned to carry out the precious Word of God that was being decreed through the spoken word!

6. Touch

Angels often communicate through touch, stroking your hair or face or placing their hands on your back or shoulder, and in this way, they provide you with a supernatural message of encouragement and strength. Sometimes, you will feel them standing by your side or behind you. One lady wrote to me: "Twice I woke up at night when someone was touching my shoulder, another time touching my foot.... I thought my husband was touching me but he was sleeping at the other side of the bed. Awakening angels 'woke me up.'" Another lady shared: "I'd be awakened by a soft touch, like the touch of a feather on my hand."

When angels want to communicate with you, it's possible to actually be touched by them. Although the Scriptures don't specify, we can imagine that when an angel appeared to strengthen Jesus (see Luke 22:43), he must have reached out and laid his hands on the Savior. When the prophet

Elijah was fleeing from Jezebel, the Bible tells us *"behold, then an angel touched him"* (1 Kings 19:5). When the angel came to Peter's rescue in his jail cell, Scripture says, *"He tapped Peter on the side and woke him up"* (Acts 12:7 BSB).

7. Hearing

Although angels can speak in any recognizable language, this method of communication seems to be the least common of all. Still, you may hear the voice of an angel trying to communicate with you. Most people are alerted to these angel messages early in the morning as they awake or late at night when preparing to sleep. When your body is at rest, your spirit is most alert.

Lois shared her testimony with me: "One night before going to bed, very discouraged, I cried out to the Lord, and that night, an angel sang in my left ear! It was amazing."

Taylor from Texas shared, "I've been awakened to hear angels singing over me. This was during an extremely tumultuous time in my life, and I felt such peace after they did that."

Angels always come with a message from heaven, but it's up to us to hear, believe, and receive what they're saying. We have heard angels singing in our meetings many times. Just recently, in Taipei, Taiwan, we heard angels singing on several occasions. In fact, this has happened every time I've spoken at this particular church over the past three years. During one meeting, we heard the sound of piano and violin being played, without any natural explanation. I believe that there is a heavenly choir and orchestra that desire to join our worship of Jesus! Music is one of the languages of angels. They were created to praise the Lord! You need to know that angels speak and that their messages *can* be received.

Our Response to Angels and Their Messages

As much as your angels want to communicate with you, it is important for you to learn how to properly respond to them. Through my research and personal interaction with angels over the years, I've discovered that there are three initial responses that people usually have to the sudden appearance of angels in their lives. These responses are much the same as the reaction people have to divine supernatural realities of any kind (i.e., visions, miracles, the moving of the Holy Spirit, etc.). None of these responses can be considered better than the others, so you need not feel ashamed by any of them.

Acceptance of the spirit world is a growing process, and we are all in training. The more you become aware of the angels who surround your life, the better you will be at accepting them, working with them, and seeing positive results on a day-to-day basis. If you've had a personal encounter with your angels, I'm sure you'll be able to relate to at least one of these three main responses.

1. Becoming Fearful

Although we were created to discover the depths of God's glory, many of us have been programmed to deny anything that is not rationally logical or reasonably explained. Because of our rigid mind-sets, we can become deeply disturbed by anything that appears to be "out of the norm." Throughout Scripture, one of the first messages that typically come from an angel's mouth is "*fear not*" or "*do not be afraid*." As humans, we often fear anything we have not experienced before.

If you've noticed a personal tendency to be afraid of spiritual things, I want to encourage you to keep 2 Timothy 1:7 close to your heart. Begin to believe it and speak it aloud: "*For God has not given us the spirit of fear; but of power, and of love, and of a sound mind.*" Your angels have been assigned to bless your life, so you have no reason to fear them. They come from God to deliver messages, bringing healing, miracles, and other good things. Let the Spirit teach you how to welcome the heavenly messengers sent to you.

An angel spoke reassurances to Daniel: "*Then said [the angel] to me, Fear not, Daniel*" (Daniel 10:12). I have noticed that fear is a common reaction to supernatural encounters. But even when our response is fear, the Lord never allows us to remain that way. He always comes with a message that says, in effect, "Fear not, for I am with you. Do not be afraid." There is always a word that comes from heaven to cause our fear to dissipate. Have you noticed that? When the angels of God show up, they will invariably tell you not to be afraid.

2. Becoming Emotionally Impacted

Some people may begin to tremble when they see an angel, or when the presence of angels is detected in the atmosphere. This can feel like butterflies fluttering around on the inside of your stomach, like a wave of electricity, or vibrations flowing up and down your body. These are all natural responses to the realm of supernatural angels.

When this unnamed angel appeared in a vision to Daniel, he was instantly drained of all his strength (see Daniel 10:8), he fell into a deep sleep (see Daniel 10:9), and he ended up propped up on his hands and knees (see Daniel 10:10). Then he began to experience trembling vibrations throughout his entire body. (See Daniel 10:11.) During this, although his companions couldn't see the angel who appeared to Daniel, they could certainly feel his presence. Scripture says they began *"quaking"* and then *"they fled to hide themselves"* (Daniel 10:7). I don't want to run away from the angels who have been assigned to my life, do you?

Your emotions have been given to you as a good gift from God, allowing you to feel spiritual realities. While it is certainly true that we walk by faith, when we do, our faith positions us to discover and feel things in the Spirit. Don't feel bad for the feelings you experience. At the same time, if you're not a "feeler," don't feel bad, because there are many other ways that angels can reach out to you. God knows what you need and He knows how to deliver His message to you in a way that you can accept, as long as you remain open to receive!

3. Remaining Calm

When an angel appeared to Peter in his prison cell, it was an amazing answer to prayer. He was bound in chains between two soldiers, awaiting death by execution, and now the Lord had sent an angel to release him from his horrible imprisonment. You would think that Peter's reaction would have been either ecstatic joy, thrilling excitement, fear for being caught in the middle of an escape, or absolute astonishment at this sudden supernatural encounter. Strangely, this was not the case.

The Scriptures don't mention any particular reaction at all in this case. It seems that Peter remained calm throughout the entire experience. At one point, the Bible even says, *"He had no idea that what the angel was doing was really happening; he thought he was seeing a vision"* (Acts 12:9 NIV).

Believe it or not, this is the reaction I've had most often when angels have presented themselves to me. I never remember feeling afraid or overly emotional in any way about seeing an angel, even when I was a child. Somehow, it has always felt normal to me. When I see angels, I feel the peace of God, and then I feel calm. It is always comforting for me to see an angel.

As I travel around the world in ministry, going from city to city, it's common for me to end up in a different hotel every night. I find it so reassuring to see angels assigned to stand by me at each hotel. Just knowing that God has sent them ahead of me helps to put me at ease.

If you're ready to start *Seeing Angels*, let's pray:

Heavenly Father, thank You for placing Your heavenly messengers in our midst. We know that they have been sent by You and for Your purposes, so help us to understand the reasons they have come and how we can better partner with them. We desire for our lines of communication to be open between heaven and earth. And we praise You for this! In Jesus's holy name, amen!

PART III

Working with Your Angels

"Every visible thing in this world is put in the charge of an angel."
—*St. Augustine*

13

Commanding Your Angels

...cause Your mighty ones to come down, O LORD.
Joel 3:11

Over a period of many years, people have often asked, "Brother Joshua, is it okay for me to command my angels?" I had always answered by saying that I didn't have a specific revelation on that subject. My understanding of how to interact with my angels was always by speaking Scriptures aloud, by prayer directed to God, and through focused generous giving. Those three things had always activated angels in my life, and I had never felt fully comfortable with the idea of directly commanding my angels in any other way. In the Psalms, David says, "*God will command his angels*" (Psalm 91:11 CEV), and I had always felt like that was the end of the story. God commands angels, not Joshua Mills.

However, everything in God is intended to be planted in our lives as a seed, and if we allow Him to sprinkle His water (the Word) upon that seed, and shine His light (the Spirit) upon it, we can expect something new to grow within us. And this is what happened to me in regard to commanding angels. The more I have sought God about these things, the more He has spoken to me regarding the rights and authority of the believer.

Proof That Angels Must Be Commanded

First, we must look into the Word of God to see if commanding our angels is even possible, and if any biblical figures from the past ever did such a thing. Some preachers would like to tell you that commanding your angels is unscriptural but I've found proof to the contrary.

Take for example the psalmist David in Psalm 103. He begins by stating: *"Bless the Lord, O my soul: and all that is within me, bless His holy name."* In that statement, he's not speaking to God or to other people; he's actually speaking to himself. And he's not merely speaking but *commanding* his own soul—mind, will, and emotions—to come into alignment and begin praising the Lord.

David continues commanding his soul until verse 20, when he suddenly commands the angels that surround him, boldly declaring, *"Bless the Lord, you His angels, that excel in strength, that do His commandments, hearkening to the voice of His word."* David was saying, in essence, "I command you angels to bless the Lord! You are powerful and you have the responsibility to carry out the desire of the Lord! When I speak God's word, you *must* listen and obey!" Wow! That's a bold statement to make! You can't possibly read that Scripture any other way. David was commanding angels and telling them to praise the Lord in the same way that he had commanded his own soul to praise God.

Now turn to Judges 6 and you will see God's mighty man of valor, Gideon, commanding an angel. This occurs when an angel suddenly appeared, sat under an oak tree, and began having a conversation with Gideon. In verses 17-18, Gideon says, *"If now I have found grace in your sight, then show me a sign that you talk with me. Depart not from here, I pray you, until I come to you, and bring forth my present, and set it before you."* Gideon literally commands the angel to stay in place until he can return with a meal of bread, meat, and soup, and sure enough, the angel responds, saying, *"I will tarry until you come again."* Gideon commanded the angel to stay, and he did!

I also want you to consider the spiritual vision that Zechariah had of Joshua, the high priest standing in the court of heaven:

Now Joshua was clothed with filthy (nauseatingly vile) garments and was standing before the Angel [of the LORD]. He spoke to those who stood before Him, saying, "Remove the filthy garments from him." And He said to Joshua, "See, I have caused your wickedness to be taken away from you, and I will clothe and beautify you with rich robes [of forgiveness]." And I (Zechariah) said, "Let them put a clean turban on his head." So they put a clean turban on his head and clothed him with [rich] garments. And the Angel of the LORD stood by.

(Zechariah 3:3–5 AMP)

It was Zechariah who commanded the angels to put the clean turban on Joshua's head, and after he spoke, the angels simply did what he asked. In this instance, we know that Zechariah was having a prophetic encounter, so this portion of Scripture gives us insight in regards to commanding our angels, even in prophetic encounters.

Jesus Christ, Himself, said something noteworthy in regards to this issue: *"Don't you realize that I could ask my Father for thousands of angels to protect us, and he would send them instantly?"* (Matthew 26:53 NLT) We know that Jesus didn't command the angels in that instance because He knew it would've impaired His journey to the cross, which was part of the assignment He had to fulfil in order to bring salvation to humanity. In other words, it would've been against the will of the Father. But when Jesus spoke these words, He gave us an insight: *"I could ask my Father for thousands of angels to protect us, and he would send them instantly."* When we ask God for anything in line with His will, He is faithful to perform His Word:

Yes, ask me for anything in my name, and I will do it!

(John 14:14 NLT)

If you remain in me and my words remain in you, you may ask for anything you want, and it will be granted! (John 15:7 NLT)

And since we know he hears us when we make our requests, we also know that he will give us what we ask for. (1 John 5:15 NLT)

Throughout Scripture, we find several biblical examples in which people—including Jesus—were able to command angels. This helps us to understand the basic principle of the spirit world concerning these ministering spirits: angels never move on their own accord. They do not look for opportunities to be utilized on their own merit. God's angels always follow the protocol of His voice. And as a believer, you have the right, responsibility, and authority to use your voice to speak God's Word.

The Believer's Authority

There is a wonderful book written many years ago by Kenneth Hagin called *The Believer's Authority*.[33] I read that book for the first time when I was about eighteen years old, and it was revolutionary. The dynamics of faith were expounded upon so powerfully in the pages of that book, I received the God-birthed revelations it contained. I quote:

"In Christ, all spiritual blessings belong to us."[34]

> *All praise to God, the Father of our Lord Jesus Christ, who has blessed us with every spiritual blessing in the heavenly realms because we are united with Christ.* (Ephesians 1:3 NLT)

"When Christ ascended, He transferred His authority to the Church. He is the Head of the Church, and believers make up the Body."[35]

> *Jesus came and told his disciples, "I have been given all authority in heaven and on earth."* (Matthew 28:18 NLT)

> *Listen carefully: I have given you authority [that you now possess] to tread on serpents and scorpions, and [the ability to exercise authority] over all the power of the enemy (Satan); and nothing will [in any way] harm you.* (Luke 10:19 AMP)

---

33. Kenneth E. Hagin, *The Believer's Authority* (Tulsa, OK: Kenneth Hagin Ministries, 1967).
34. Ibid, 12.
35. Ibid, 19.

"Christ is seated at the right hand of the Father—the place of authority—and we're seated with Him."[36]

> *But God is so rich in mercy, and he loved us so much, that even though we were dead because of our sins, he gave us life when he raised Christ from the dead. (It is only by God's grace that you have been saved!) For he raised us from the dead along with Christ and seated us with him in the heavenly realms because we are united with Christ Jesus.*
>
> (Ephesians 2:4–6 NLT)

When I read those Scriptures as a teenager, I received an impartation of bold faith to move with God in the areas of healing, finances, and miracles. These Scriptures gave me great confidence, knowing that the power and authority of God resided in me through Christ Jesus. But when it came to commanding angels, I still wasn't sure, and it seemed to be a controversial subject among believers. Did I really believe that God had given us all power and authority? Many believers didn't think it was possible. But wasn't that the Word of God? Had His Word to us changed? Certainly not. So, if God's Word had not changed, then what needed to change was my understanding of it.

New Covenant Privileges

The Bible tells us to rightly divide the Word (see 2 Timothy 2:15) so that we can clearly gain truthful insight of our rights and privileges in Christ. Before Jesus went to the cross, He was made a little lower than the angels. (See Psalm 8:5; Hebrews 2:7.) But now, on this side of the cross, He has been crowned with glory and honor so that the angels must submit to His name. (See Hebrews 2:9; Philippians 2:10). And look at these Scriptures:

> *I also pray that you will understand the incredible greatness of God's power for us who believe him. This is the same mighty power that raised Christ from the dead and seated him in the place of honor at God's right hand in the heavenly realms. Now he is far above any ruler or authority or power or leader or anything else—not only in this world but also in the world to come.* (Ephesians 1:19–21 NLT)

---

36. Ibid.

Now Christ has gone to heaven. He is seated in the place of honor next to God, and all the angels and authorities and powers accept his authority.

(1 Peter 3:22 NLT)

It seems plain to see that angels are subject to Christ. Thus, let me ask you this: Where is Christ? Where does He live right now? The answer is discovered in Colossians 1:27:

And this is the secret: Christ lives in you. This gives you assurance of sharing his glory.

(NLT)

Christ lives in you and Christ lives in me. We have the privilege of sharing in His glory! This gives you the right to speak by the authority of Christ, who lives in you. You possess spiritual authority to invoke God's Word and command angels to move in your life.

Speaking by the Authority of Christ

When you speak by the authority of Christ, who resides in you, the spirit world pays attention. Your words are powerful and full of God's authority. When you speak by the Spirit, it is God who is speaking. (See Luke 12:12.) You must understand this.

The Spirit of God spoke to Charles Capps one day, sharing with him some secrets about angels and the way they operate on behalf of mankind. The Lord said:

One reason the words you speak are so important is because the angels are listening to what you say.... They stand beside you daily, listening to the words that come out of your mouth. If your words are in line with My Word, then the angels go to work immediately, causing the things you speak to come to pass. But if you speak things that are contrary to My Word, you won't get an audience with angels. They won't operate on those words.... They are designed as ministering spirits to minister for you.... You should always speak in line with My Word in order for My will to come to pass in your life.[37]

---

37. Charles and Annette Capps, *Angels: Knowing Their Purpose, Releasing Their Power* (Tulsa, OK: Harrison House, 1984).

Through these words, the Spirit reminds us today that angels listen to our voices and our words, as they are spoken in accordance with God's will—which, we know, is His Word. Jesus said, *"Whosoever shall confess Me before men, him shall the Son of man also confess before the angels of God"* (Luke 12:8). In other words, when we confess that Jesus is our Lord, He confesses it back to the angels. He declares to them what we have first declared. When we speak by the authority of Christ, it sets angels into action.

Who Is the Commander of the Army of the Lord?

Since we know that many of God's angels are called "hosts" or "mighty ones," speaking in military terms of a great army, the question remains: Who is the Commander of this army? Who is the Commander of the army of the Lord? We find the answer in Joshua 5:

The commander of the LORD's army replied, "Take off your sandals, for the place where you are standing is holy." And Joshua did as he was told.   (Joshua 5:15 NLT)

In this passage, we see Joshua taking off his sandals and bowing down to worship the Commander. This couldn't possibly have been just another angel because, throughout the Scriptures, we see that the worship of angels is forbidden, and yet Joshua seemed to be permitted to worship in this way. The Commander of the Lord's army is Jesus Himself, and He wants to give voice to His commands through you and me.

I believe that God is telling us today the same thing that He told Moses so long ago: *"Now therefore go, and I will be with your mouth, and teach you what you shall say"* (Exodus 4:12).

We must have confidence that God wants to dispatch angels at our Spirit-led commands to minister for us. You can make decrees and the angels will respond.

Command Your Angels to Help You

Janet and I practice commanding our angels every day, to help us with the tasks at hand. And when we ask them to help, it's amazing how quickly they do just that! Just the other day, as I was traveling home on an overseas flight after ministering in Tokyo, I received a text message from Janet while in the sky. She told me that she had been struggling in an attempt to open a computer program after downloading the newer software update on her laptop. At this point, she had already spent two hours to no avail. She was desperate for help and she was reaching out to ask me for prayer. When I received this request, God quickened my spirit to command angels on Janet's behalf, to help her solve this technical problem. Now some skeptics may be quick to criticize my attempts but you cannot argue with the evidence! Within seconds of commanding those angels, Janet wrote back and said, "Wow! I opened it, not kidding! It worked! Praise God!"

If I can command my angels thousands of miles away on an airplane, you can do it too! It works—it really does!

Command Your Angels by Speaking a Blessing

One of the ways I enjoy commanding the angels over my children's lives is by speaking a daily blessing over them. Dr. Mary Ruth Swope has provided a wonderful decree for this in her anointed book, *The Power of Blessing Your Children*. I would encourage you to speak it over your loved ones too:

> In the name of Jesus Christ:
>
> I bless you with a host of active angels whom God made to guard and rescue all who reverence Him. He will send these ministering spirits to protect His children from danger and to defend them from their enemies.
>
> Your angels in heaven have constant access to Your heavenly Father, and He orders them to protect you wherever you go. Throughout your life, they will steady you with their hands to keep you from stumbling over the stones along your pathway.
>
> Do not be afraid; unseen warriors walk beside you.[38]

There are several different ways in which you can command your angels but the most important aspect of asking is always to remember to

---

38. Mary Ruth Swope, *The Power of Blessing Your Children* (New Kensington, PA: Whitaker House, 1992, 2010), 35.

command them using the name of Jesus. This is the authority we use in the realm of the Spirit.

If you're ready to start *Seeing Angels*, let's pray:

Father, I believe what You have told us in Your Word. I accept the authority You have given me to act in Your name. Therefore, with confidence, I speak to the angels You have assigned to my life and command them to minister, as they were intended, to every need of my life. In Jesus's name, Amen!

14

Understanding Angel Signs and Heavenly Messages

Speak, Lord; for Your servant hears.
1 Samuel 3:9

Several years ago, I was in Nashville to record songs for my holiday album called *Christmas Miracle*. On the first day of recording, I was working with my producer in his home studio to lay down the vocal tracks for the song "Angels from the Realms of Glory," when out of his studio window I saw his fifteen-foot trampoline flying solo through the air. It soared over his house and landed in the front yard. That full-size trampoline had been lifted over his house without damaging the roof, the perimeter fence, or any of the other nearby homes, before making a perfect pinpoint landing in the front yard. This had never happened to them before and has never happened since. None of his neighbors have ever had it happen. In fact, nobody around them had ever heard of such a thing happening without a tornado destroying everything.

We immediately ran outside to see if we could rescue the trampoline before it was damaged—or before it damaged something else! Between three grown men, we were not able to lift it, so we struggled and strained to roll it around the house and into the backyard.

Why am I telling all of this? Keep in mind that one of God's names for angels is "winds," and I have discovered that angels don't always do what you expect them to do. Sometimes they do things just to get your attention so that you can recognize they are present in your life—on the scene and available to assist you.

Angels are some of the most unrecognized ministers of God on the face of the earth, and this should not be. If we can learn how to recognize angels and their signs, it will position us to receive the messages they bring. Through that encounter in Nashville, I clearly understood that God was assigning angels from the realms of glory over that album project. Just knowing that fact gave me both peace and confidence as I continued to walk through the process of financing, recording, releasing, and distributing the album. Angels had been dispatched from heaven and assigned over that project. Because God's hand has rested upon *Christmas Miracle*, many people have been blessed by it.

Of course, you won't always see flying trampolines when angels are present. More often the signs are much more subtle.

Heavenly Fragrance

There are times when various fragrances will come with the presence of angels, and the particular fragrance may indicate the ministry function or give us an understanding of the particular message our heavenly messengers are bringing to us as they administrate God's purposes in our business, ministry, or life.

While I was ministering in Rhode Island, the scent of baby powder permeated the air during the service. This would have been very easy to dismiss because it's such a common smell. We may say things like, "That's weird," "I wonder where that's coming from," "that's very unusual," or "how strange." Then we brush it off and go on as if nothing has happened. At the same time, we know that God wants to give us signs and wonders. Unusual smells may be an indicator that God is delivering messages through the angels who are coming and going, hovering over us, and ministering in our midst, and yet, we can be spiritually blind to all of it. It shouldn't be that way, and God doesn't want it to be that way. His desire is to teach us to see, to hear, and to perceive. He even wants us to taste His goodness.

What was the baby powder all about? It just so happened that there was a couple there who were believing God to have children. When that baby powder smell came, it was their word from the Lord. God was speaking to them, saying that babies were on the way.

Baby powder is also so fresh. It indicates something new. Can you smell it? What does it mean? Some of you need that message, and it's a message from heaven to you right now. Babies are on the way! This represents all of the new things God is wanting to do. There have been many obstacles and delays in the natural, but today, right now, God says that babies are on the way.

I can feel that miracle realm right now. I can feel the miracles dropping down on us. Things that have been impossible in the natural are becoming absolutely possible in the glory. Your faith is beginning to connect. Reach up into the glory realms, the unseen, and receive the miracle you need. Take it right now.

Through the years, I have discovered that the divine supernatural realm is a "signs realm." Once you learn how to read, perceive, and notice the signs, you will suddenly begin to encounter this realm all around you, almost everywhere you go. God loves to send us signs, tokens of His love, and I believe that He often sends them to us through the ministry of angels.

Sometimes, for instance, when angels begin moving around us, we notice a heavenly fragrance that begins to fill the atmosphere. When this happens, it's common for the aroma to fill the entire meeting place. We've smelled the fragrance of smoke from a burning fire, which I believe prophetically represents sacrifice. More often, we've smelled the fragrance of roses, which is the fragrance of Christ Himself.

Some may wonder if it is really possible for God to minister in this way. Just read 2 Corinthians 2:14:

> But thanks be to God, who always leads us as captives in Christ's triumphal procession and uses us to spread the aroma of the knowledge of him everywhere.   (NIV)

This Scripture tells us clearly that God will use us to spread the aroma of Christ everywhere. But, since we are partnered with our angels, it should be no surprise that God would also choose to use the angels in this way as well.

Scriptural Fragrance Chart		
Type	Scriptures	Description
Calamus	• Exodus 30:23 • Ezekiel 27:19 • Isaiah 43:24 • Jeremiah 6:20	• Sweet Cane • Used in sacred anointing oil • Precious perfume
Cedar	• Psalm 92:12 • Psalm 104:16 • Isaiah 41:9 • Ezekiel 31:3	• Great Strength & Might • Aromatic odor (offensive to insects) • Evergreen (Long-life) • Watered Abundantly • Wilderness • S.A.P. (Supernatural Anointing for Prosperity)
Cinnamon	• Exodus 30:23 • Proverbs 7:17 • Song of Solomon 4:14	• Used in sacred anointing oil • A perfume for a bed
Frankincense	• Exodus 30:34-35 • Leviticus 2:1-2 • Nehemiah 13:5 • Psalm 141:2 • Malachi 1:11 • Matthew 2:11	• Perfume of the sanctuary • Pure and holy • Offering of sacrifice • Consecrated dedication • Emblem of prayer • Symbol of the divine name

Scriptural Fragrance Chart

Type	Scriptures	Description
Honey	• Exodus 3:6-8 • Exodus 16:31 • 1 Samuel 14:24-27 • Psalm 119:103 • Proverbs 24:13 • Revelations 10:7-11	• God's inspired Word • Promised land/territory • Abundance, ease and prosperity • Sweet and delightful • Good health • Miracles
Lily of the Valley	• Song of Solomon 2:1; 2:2; 6:2 • Hosea 14:5 • Matthew 6:28	• The love of God • The fragrance of Christ • Accelerated growth • Supernatural prosperity • God's loving care and concern
Myrrh	• Genesis 37:25; 43:11 • Exodus 30:23 • Psalm 45:8 • Proverbs 7:17 • Luke 24:1	• Used in the sacred anointing oil • Honored gift • Transition
Rose of Sharon (also connected to the aroma of other fragrant flowers)	• Song of Solomon 2:1	• The fragrance of Christ • Unfolding wisdom • Spiritual joy • Comfort • Divine love • The miracle of life

Scriptural Fragrance Chart		
Type	Scriptures	Description
Saffron	• Song of Solomon 4:14	• Beauty • Great worth • Zest for life
Smoke (Burning Fire)	• Exodus 19:18; 20:18 • Isaiah 4:5; 6:4 • Acts 2:3 • Revelations 8:4; 15:8	• The glory of God • The power of God • New move of God
Spikenard (also called Nard)	• Song of Solomon 1:12; 4:14 • Mark 14:3 • John 12:3,5	• Precious perfume • Preparation • High value/genuine • Worship

My friend Pastor Timothy Stevenson, who leads a great church in Auckland, New Zealand, has been learning how to cooperate with his angels and understand the messages they bring through heavenly fragrances. I asked him to share some of his insights:

> My journey into the glory realm and learning to work with the angels has taken place over many years. A lot of my learning has come through cause-and-effect type encounters. Although I have experienced many different aromas in meetings, over a period of time I began to recognize a particularly strong but beautiful aroma that is difficult to describe. What I noticed was that every time I smelled that aroma, the supernatural would always manifest. There would be miracles, signs, and wonders such as healings and the appearance of drops of oil and gold flakes. Then, I finally got it! It was an angel!
>
> Now I know that this angel often travels with me, and what I have come to realize is that every time I smell his presence, I know

to step out and believe for signs, wonders, and miracles. Sometimes, I will walk into our church on a Sunday morning and will "bump into" him on the way to my seat. I step into his aroma and know that he is there. When this happens, I know that God's glory will manifest through the supernatural.

Often, the angel will manifest through his aroma during praise and worship. When this happens, I make space for the Holy Spirit so that the supernatural can take place. He also manifests while I am preaching, and then I will stop and make decrees, for this angel also brings breakthrough—especially in the realm of finances.

The big lesson I have learned is that this angel always manifests for a purpose: to manifest the glory of heaven. Therefore, I have to be obedient and make space for the supernatural when he does, so that Jesus is fully glorified.

Sometimes, the Lord allows us to smell the fragrance of angels, and at other times, He allows them to bring other signs that help us to know they are near.

Finding Angel Feathers

When our angels want to deliver a message, one sign they commonly give us is the appearance of feathers. Often, these feathers are small, white, and delicate, and they usually appear in a special place at a special time. But that's exactly the reason it grabs our attention!

Some people have asked me if angels really have wings with feathers, and my answer is yes, they do. The Scriptures speak about the wings of an angel. Psalm 18:10, for instance, says, *"He rode upon a cherub, and did fly: yea, He did fly upon the wings of the wind."* When the psalmist considered the faithful protection of God over our lives, he sang, *"He will shelter you with his wings. His faithful promises are your armor and protection"* (Psalm 91:4 NLT).

God will cover you with whose wings? As I mentioned before, God Himself does not have wings but the angels He created do, and they work as one in spirit with God to accomplish His divine purposes. Because you are a believer, He has promised to cover your life with angelic protection, and He created His host of angels with you in mind. We can understand this scriptural passage more fully when we see that the psalmist later sang, *"He will command his angels concerning you to guard you in all your ways"* (Psalm 91:11 NIV).

Feathers are spiritually symbolic of God's faithfulness, protection, and covenant promises, and they help us rise above difficulties. (See Exodus 25:20; Psalm 63:7.) Feathers are also a sign that God is bringing swift answers to prayers and accelerating the manifestation of His blessings in your life. (See Deuteronomy 32:10–12.)

Still, some people wonder, "Can angel feathers really manifest in the natural dimension? And what do they look like?" Well, we know for certain that God chooses to release spiritual realities on the earth in a natural sort of way. Our faith moves heaven to earth. When Jesus taught us to pray, He said to say: *"Your kingdom come. Your will be done in earth, as it is in heaven"* (Matthew 6:10). There are times when heaven will literally begin to appear around us in the natural. That's what God desires.

But you may still be asking the question: "What should these feathers look like?" We can find an answer for this, once again, revealed in the Scriptures: *"Then I looked up and saw two women flying toward us, gliding on the wind. They had wings like a stork"* (Zechariah 5:9 NLT). This passage is speaking specifically about two-winged female spirits. Scholars have debated whether or not they were angels, but I think we can agree that if we saw these spirit beings with our own eyes, we would certainly assume they were angels. What I want you to notice here is that this Scripture describes their wings as being *"like a stork."* A stork's average wingspan is seventy-three inches (more than six feet), and its plumage is mainly white, with some black on the wings.[39]

This revelation about the angels' wings gives us an understanding of their feathers. Therefore, when we see angel's feathers, we would expect them to look similar to the feathers of a bird. As I noted, angel feathers are often white, but sometimes they appear to be black or some other color altogether. Each color has a different prophetic symbolism and you should

39. See James A. Hancock, *Storks, Ibises, and Spoonbills of the World* (Cambridge, MA: Academic Press, 1992).

apply that knowledge if and when you notice that your angel's feathers are of different colors. For that purpose, I have prepared a scriptural color chart, which can be found at the end of this chapter.

Heavenly messages often come to us like a code and we are given the privileged opportunity to search out their meanings. The Bible says plainly: *"It is God's privilege to conceal things and the king's privilege to discover them"* (Proverbs 25:2 NLT). Sometimes, angel feathers may even appear with a unique pattern or in an unusual shape. One of my friends received a feather that was in a spiral shape. The Lord spoke to him clearly through that encounter about childlike faith and the miracles it produces.

Sometimes, God will provide you with a message inside of another message. This is why it is imperative to use godly discernment and consult the Holy Spirit regarding each and every manifestation. We must pay attention to the signs God gives when He is sending us a message through His angels.

Angel Signs Confirm the Message in Austria

The Bible tells us that one of the main reasons God allows us to see angel signs is because it is a confirmation of His Word. We don't believe His Word because we see signs; rather we see signs of heaven all around us because we *choose* to believe God's Word by faith.

The first evening I was ministering with Pastor Elisabeth Lindenthaler in Graz, Austria, my spiritual eyes were opened to see seven large angels standing across the platform. I believe these were the same seven angels who stand in the glory of God. I told the people present what I was seeing because I believed it was an invitation from the Lord to enter into His throne room.

Later that evening and into the next morning, as I was ministering, I kept noticing feathers falling through the air and landing directly on the open pages of my Bible. They were so large and noticeable that I picked them up to show my translator, who was standing beside me. She also noticed feathers falling around her. God was giving us another sign of the presence of His angels. This greatly impacted the people who were present in those meetings. They felt so encouraged and uplifted in their faith just knowing that God had sent His heavenly company to surround our time together.

"He Shall Cover You with His Feathers"

In another gathering near Rockford, Illinois, God gave me prophetic eyes to see His angels filling the room. There was a lady in attendance who wasn't quite sure about the validity of the visitation I was having because she had not yet felt it in that same way. As she sought the Spirit and asked Him to reveal the truth to her, tiny feathers began appearing all around her chair. It was quite amazing! The Scriptures declare that when you enter God's secret place, *"He shall cover you with His feathers"* (Psalm 91:4), and that is exactly what happened!

As I was speaking about the ministry service of angels at Dr. Mahesh and Bonnie Chavda's All Nations Church, in Fort Mill, South Carolina, I kept noticing tiny feathers floating down in the air in front of me. I couldn't ignore it. Every once in a while, about two feet in front of me and three feet over my head, I noticed a single, white, quarter-inch feather fluttering in the air. I knew that this was a sign of confirmation—that what I was saying was being affirmed by God with a heavenly sign. I also knew that the angels I was speaking about were present and ministering according to the word I was sharing.

Remember, the Bible says that signs confirm the Word. (See Mark 16:20.) Most people in attendance weren't able to see what I was seeing because the feathers were so tiny. Even though a few people in the front row noticed them as well, this was a personal sign meant for me, assuring me that I was leading them in the right direction.

I stopped for a moment, thanked God for this angel sign, and then continued to speak with boldness, knowing that I had heaven's approval. This stamp of divine approval restores our confidence and encourages us to go deeper in the things of God. In that meeting, I invited people to come forward to receive prayer and a special impartation. It was a powerful time. One lady told me that it was the most powerful meeting she had ever attended in which she had felt the activation of the angelic realm.

Later that day, while speaking with Dr. Mahesh about these things, he mentioned to me that there have been several other times in that church when a flurry of thousands of feathers have fallen at one time. They have those moments recorded on video. It is exciting to see the ways in which God's angels can manifest themselves all around us!

Angels Leave a Calling Card in New Zealand

While ministering in Auckland, New Zealand, my sister, Sabrina, stayed behind at the hotel to watch Lincoln, who was only an infant at the time. During the meetings, the Holy Spirit had been teaching us a lot about angels. We would study the Bible, find Scriptures about the ways in which they moved, and then we saw them manifest openly in our midst. It was wonderful!

When we arrived back at the hotel that night, Sabrina said, "Lincoln's upstairs sleeping if you want to go see him." It had been hot in the room, so Sabrina had taken off Lincoln's shirt and let him sleep without it. Now, as we entered the room and looked at him, we saw that there were four feathers perfectly arranged side-by-side on his chest. Only weeks before that, the Lord had shown me the four angels who He had assigned over our son, and now, those angels had left their calling cards for us to find. It was another natural indicator of a spiritual reality. Not only was Sabrina watching over Lincoln, but his angels were watching over him too, and that brought us great comfort.

God wants to show us these things, but our eyes must to be open to see them. We could have walked into that room, seen the four feathers, and imagined that they had come out of the pillow he was sleeping on. If you want to, you can dismiss any miracle:

"Well, yes, I thought I was healed last night, but it could have been only a coincidence that the pain in my foot went away."

"Maybe my condition wasn't as serious as I thought it was in the first place."

"The migraine was probably going to stop bothering me on its own."

You can either have faith and believe in what God is doing or you can make up any sort of excuse to dismiss His wonders as being something totally natural and ordinary. Oh, how He wants you to have eyes to see and a heart to receive His messages from heaven!

Decoding Angel Signs and Understanding Their Meaning

On face value, angel signs can be easily explained away if we don't have the prophetic understanding to know that God is attempting to speak to us through these signs. Our angels want us to receive God's message, and they will do everything possible to present it to us. But, as I've shown, we must first become aware of the signs of their presence, and, second, we must take the time to ask ourselves some specific questions about those signs.

One of the first things an investigative journalist is taught during their training period is the "Six W's." When I observe an angel feather falling around me or appearing in an unusual way, I ask myself the following five "W" questions: who, what, where, when, why, and how?

1. **Who** was I thinking about or praying for at that time or just before this sign appeared? (Hint: It might be a relative, a close friend, people from a certain church service, etc.)

2. **What** were my initial feelings, thoughts, or impressions when the feather or feathers first appeared? (Hint: This includes feelings of joy, relief, strength, encouragement, etc.)

3. **Where** did the feather appear? (Hint: It might have been in a doorway, in a child's bedroom, in a wallet, etc. Does the place hold any particular or prophetic significance for you?)

4. **When** did this sign appear? (Hint: This includes the day of the week, month, year, or time on the clock, etc. It is very important to take note of the prophetic numbers and patterns connected to the message.)

5. **Why** did this sign appear at this time? (Hint: Has anything in particular been troubling you or been of great concern to you? How have you been feeling spiritually, emotionally, and physically?)

6.   *How* did this sign appear? (Hint: Was it sudden or gradual? Did you detect any other signs?)

You can use these same questions when examining any God-sent sign that comes to you, whether it be in heavenly fragrances, orbs of lights, golden glory, supernatural oil, etc. These questions will be helpful for you to zero-in and correctly understand the specific message that is being communicated. Of course, all of these questions should be asked in combination with spiritual discernment and common sense, as well as through the lens of our personal relationship with Jesus Christ, in order for us to determine the full meaning of the messages we're receiving.

A Scriptural Understanding of Colors

In the beginning, God introduced our world to color when He released His light into the universe. Yes, color was His idea. He is the Master Artist, and through His artwork, He conveys thoughts, ideas, and messages. I don't believe that God does anything by accident, but each and every part of His creation carries a God-ordained message. In my book, *Atmosphere,*[40] I've shared about the emotional impact colors can make upon a person's physical and mental well-being, but there is also a spiritual side to the color spectrum. There is a prophetic edge that we must become aware of. Through color, God can speak to us about healing, spiritual growth, redemption, or any number of other things. When we begin to receive visible angel signs and messages from heaven, we should take note of the colors that we see. I have compiled a chart and inserted it here to help you understand the positive meaning of colors, according to the Scriptures.

---

40. Joshua Mills, *Atmosphere* (Palm Springs, CA: New Wine International, 2011).

Scriptural Color Chart		

White	• Isaiah 1:18
	• John 4:35;
	  1 Corinthians 6:11;
	  Ephesians 5:26
	• Ephesians 5:25;
	  1 Corinthians 13
	• Daniel 7:9; Matthew
	  28:3; Mark 9:3;
	  Revelation 1:14
	• John 4:35
		• Purity
		• Sanctification
		• Godly love
		• The image of Christ
		• Harvest

Black	• Exodus 28:9–12, 35:27 • Zechariah 6:2–6	• Governmental authority • Righteous judgment

Red	• Leviticus 17:11;
	  Hebrews 11:28; 1 John
	  1:9; 2 Corinthians 5:21
	• Matthew 27:28;
	  Colossians 1:20–21
		• The blood of Jesus
		• Salvation
		• The healing of
		  mankind (from the
		  Hebrew word *oudem*)

Orange	• Psalm 2:9; Revelation
	  19:15
	• Exodus 24:17; Hebrews
	  12:29
	• Acts 2:3–4
	• Daniel 10:6; Revelation
	  1:14, 2:18
		• Breakthrough
		• The fire of God
		• The "new"
		• The eyes of God

Yellow	• Isaiah 60:6 • Revelation 21:19–20 • Ezekiel 1:16, 10:9	• A special gift • Perfection • Turning things around

Scriptural Color Chart

Green	<ul><li>Genesis 1:11–13, 2:8, 15</li><li>Psalm 1:3, 52:8</li><li>Psalm 92:12, 14</li><li>Jeremiah 11:16, 17:8; Hosea 14:8</li><li>Psalm 23:2–3</li></ul>	<ul><li>Growth/new beginnings</li><li>Immortality/everlasting life</li><li>Prosperity</li><li>Good fruit</li><li>Peace/restoration</li></ul>
Blue	<ul><li>Numbers 15:38–41</li><li>John 6:31, 33, 38</li><li>Exodus 27:16</li><li>Exodus 24:10; Ezekiel 1:26, 10:1</li><li>Isaiah 54:11</li><li>Matthew 9:21</li></ul>	<ul><li>The Word of God/revelation</li><li>Heaven</li><li>The righteousness of God</li><li>The throne of God</li><li>Laying proper foundations</li><li>Wholeness</li></ul>
Violet/Purple	<ul><li>John 2</li><li>Proverbs 3:10</li><li>Judges 8:26; Esther 8:15</li><li>Luke 16:19; Acts 16:14</li></ul>	<ul><li>Miracles</li><li>Overflow</li><li>Royalty</li><li>Wealth/prosperity/luxury</li></ul>
Gold	<ul><li>1 Peter 1:7</li><li>Job 23:10</li><li>Revelation 3:18</li><li>Exodus 25:10–21; Hebrews 9:4</li></ul>	<ul><li>Faith</li><li>Purification</li><li>Refinement</li><li>The glory of God</li></ul>
Silver	<ul><li>Psalm 66:10; Matthew 27:3–10; 1 Peter 1:18–19</li><li>Psalm 12:6</li><li>Genesis 13:2</li></ul>	<ul><li>Redemption</li><li>Truth</li><li>Riches</li></ul>
Brown	<ul><li>Isaiah 11:1</li></ul>	<ul><li>Completion/the end of a season</li></ul>

You will notice that sometimes the meanings of these colors overlap in the Scriptures. When considering these colors, you may also want to ask yourself the following questions:

- What is my personal connection to this color? (i.e., personal memories, past experiences, or emotional attachments, etc.)

- How does this color make me feel? (i.e., it brings me joy, excitement, comfort, peace, etc.)

- What do the Scriptures say about this color, and how does it apply to my current situation?

Once you have started looking, you'll begin to see the angel signs and messages from heaven almost everywhere you go! Keep your spiritual senses alert, and be ready to decode the information you receive as a gift from the glory realm!

If you're ready to start *Seeing Angels*, let's pray:

Heavenly Father, I can see signs of Your glory everywhere I look! You fill my life with the fragrance of Your love and the colors of Your majesty! Thank You for teaching me how to understand the signs that You are showing me through Your angels. And help me to accept the heavenly messages You're sending. In Jesus's name, amen!

15

Angel Movements and Atmospheric Shifts

You commandeered winds as messengers,
appointed fire and flame as ambassadors...
Psalm 104:4 (MSG)

Sometimes angels come as spirit winds (see Ezekiel 37:9; John 3:8; Acts 2:2), and at other times, they appear as seraphim or servant flames of fire (see 2 Kings 2:11, 6:17; Hebrews 1:7). As I mentioned before, you will often feel an atmospheric shift, even in the room temperature, when the hosts of angels begin to move in your midst. Those are the flames of fire in operation. Pray into the encounter and ask God what He is doing and how you can cooperate with Him in that moment.

Often, when angels begin moving in your atmosphere, you will feel something like electricity in your hands or other parts of your physical body. At other times, you may get almost the opposite manifestation and feel completely numb. These are natural indicators that something supernatural is happening. Become sensitive to these clues, and when they begin happening, ask God what He wants to reveal to you at that moment.

It could be that God is purifying something in your life. When He wanted to cleanse the prophet Isaiah, He sent an angel to touch his mouth with a flaming coal. (See Isaiah 6:6–7.) On the other hand, you may feel a cool breeze blowing across your fingertips as you lift your hands in worship. Thank God for His angels, who bring us refreshing encounters.

When angels begin to move, you will sense them shifting the atmosphere all around you. Consider these biblical examples:

+ An angel appeared in Peter's prison cell and *"a light shined in the prison"* (Acts 12:7).

+ Angels appeared to the shepherds in the fields of Judea, and suddenly *"the glory of the Lord shone round about them"* (Luke 2:9).

+ Cornelius saw the angel as *"a man in shining clothes"* (Acts 10:30).

Although it may seem doubtful that you'd ever miss the movement of angels in their shining, shimmering, and glory atmosphere, I can tell you from personal experience that, at times, it takes keen insight and sharp discernment to accurately tune into what they're doing and the ways in which they are moving. Sometimes, our own minds would like to quietly disqualify the experience or find natural excuses for the ways in which angels are moving in our lives.

Angelic Impartation in Arizona

I had an angelic encounter a few years ago while ministering in Phoenix, Arizona. During the meeting, I began to notice a heat sensation come over my body. I believe it was the fire of God, which was accompanied by the seraphim. God was working something new in me personally, but He was also giving that sign to me as an impartation to release to others.

I had never experienced such an intensity of God's fire in my life, and it came to the point that it seemed virtually impossible for me to continue to stand and speak. It felt as though I had to release the fire or it would kill me. I invited the several hundred people in attendance to quickly form prayer lines, and I began releasing the fire to them. The things that God did that night were beyond amazing. Several people were set free from the power of addictions, many people received healings in their bodies (as sickness was burned up), and one man even told me later that he could feel "the fire burning" for more than six months afterward. The impartation was that strong. I was accompanied by angels of fire the entire evening as I moved through those prayer lines, and it seemed that the more fire I gave out, the more fire I received in return.

After I had laid my hands on the last person in line, I felt I needed to rest because the fire was burning inside of me with such great intensity. I went to my hotel room and lay down on the sofa, and the entire room became flooded with the light of God's presence. The light was so bright I couldn't open my eyes. As I rested in that glory realm, I felt two angels being sent to hover over me in ministry. As they flapped their wings, I felt a cool breeze blowing across my face and arms. It was one of the most powerful impartations I have ever received from the Spirit.

In the days that followed, God opened new opportunities for our ministry, for He knew that I would need this impartation in order to walk into them fully. I am so thankful for the ministry of angels and for the way God chooses to take care of His children.

Radiant Lights and Swirling Colors

Occasionally, the Lord allows us to encounter His angels as brilliant shining lights. You might see an unusual spark of light in your peripheral vision, from the corner of your eye, a flash of lightning, or an orb of light above you, within your field of vision. These are all indicators of angel movement around you. Pay attention to these movements and consult the Holy Spirit for His wisdom. The Bible says that God is the Father of these heavenly lights. (See James 1:17.)

One summer, I had the opportunity to preach in Williamsburg, Virginia. I was traveling with Janet and Lincoln, who was quite young at the time. We had never ministered at this particular church before, and as soon as we walked into the sanctuary, Lincoln looked up and said, "Dad, I see angels all over this church!" I didn't see them, but I was thankful that he did.

"What do they look like?" I asked him.

He said all that he could see were bright orbs of swirling color. I had seen these in the past, and many other people had told me that they had seen them too. I had heard some say that these were angels, but for some reason, I never felt quite right about it. I knew that these orbs were connected to angels, but I never felt like they were angels themselves. That day in Virginia, I consulted the Spirit about it. The Spirit said, "What you are seeing is the gift and impartation." Suddenly it all made sense. The swirling colors represented the gift the angels were bringing to us.

I asked Lincoln, "What colors do you see?"

He said, "I see blue, red, and green."

This was extremely helpful for me because now I understood what God wanted to do in that meeting. He had sent His angels to help; all I needed to do was cooperate with them. I had a quickening in my spirit that blue represented prophetic revelation, red represented healing, and green represented new growth and provision. When I ministered according to what Lincoln had seen supernaturally, and what had been revealed to me spiritually, the results were wonderful! We must pay attention to atmospheric shifts and angel movements. These angels have been sent to help us—if we'll learn how to partner with them.

Angels Caught on Camera

A few years ago, I was teaching about angels at a Glory School I was hosting on the Gold Coast of Australia. I saw an angel appear in the back of the room and stand there, leaning against the wall. I could see the outline of his head but I couldn't see his face clearly. I could see his neck and shoulders. He was so tall that his head nearly touched the ceiling of the auditorium.

When I told everyone what I was seeing, the students turned around to look. Some saw the angel but most could not see it. One man later testified that he had been thinking to himself, *I really wish I could see that angel. Brother Joshua said that it's right behind me.* Then he got an idea. He took out his camera and snapped a selfie, being sure to include the area where I had said the angel was standing. He had not been able to see the angel with his natural eyes but when he looked at the photo he had taken, there it was, right behind him, exactly where I had said it was. He now had a selfie with an angel! This was encouraging to the man, instantly increasing his faith to believe God for the realms of glory. When angels show up, get your smartphone out and take photos of them. Later, you may see things in the photo that you didn't notice at the time.

Something similar happened in Taichung, Taiwan, while I was ministering there several years ago. During worship, an angel visibly appeared on the platform. This angel was dressed in glowing white linen. I didn't see the angel myself; my eyes were closed in worship. One man at the meeting also had the idea of taking a photo, and I'm so glad he did. He perfectly captured this heavenly being worshiping in our midst.

I have many photos of angels that I enjoy showing to people, and I believe that God wants to give you some of your own photos of angels!

Rainbows of Light

There is a beautiful oasis that we love to visit in Palm Springs, California. I call it the "open portal." Although it's located in the desert, it has a spectacular sixty-foot waterfall surrounded by a most peaceful and natural setting. It is a place where I love to pray and connect with God. When I go there, I can feel the presence of the Lord, and I sense the movement of angels, just as Jacob did in Genesis 28.

Some special and historic things have taken place in that location over the years, things which have changed the course of history for the church. I have noticed that there is an angel who stands resident in that place. We can always sense him spiritually, but often we can see his presence, as he wears a rainbow around his head or around his waist, like a belt. The rainbow is a sign of eternal covenant, everlasting promises, and God's faithfulness to humanity, but it can also be a sign of the presence of angels.

Some people have the mistaken concept that halos were only the invention of medieval artists as a way of indicating saints and angels in their paintings. Actually, the Bible speaks of real halos. We see an instance of this in Revelation 10:1:

Then I saw another mighty angel coming down from heaven. He was robed in a cloud, with a rainbow above his head; his face was like the sun, and his legs were like fiery pillars.   (Revelation 10:1 NIV)

Later in the chapter, this angel said, *"There will be no more delay!"* (verse 6). I have personally discovered that when the angelic realm begins to make itself known on the physical plane, God often sends a message of *"no more delay"* and *"quick acceleration"* for the answers and manifestations needed in any given situation.

There are angels of acceleration, angels who even now are declaring, "No more delay!" They are making that declaration over your life. I join them in declaring even now through the pages of this book: **"No more delay!"** Where there has been hesitation, let there be no more hesitation. Where there has been resistance, let there be no more resistance. Where there has been enemy interference, let there be no more enemy interference. **"No more delay!"** Let there be divine acceleration into the calling and the purposes of God, and into the things He has called and planned and purposed for you personally.

For those who will receive it, these angels will be attracted to your faith and will latch on to you. Then they will go with you and prepare you for more. Get ready! Get ready to see doors opened as never before! Get ready for unexpected "suddenlies"!

For some of you, God has already been ministering to your spirit. He has already been stirring something up within you, and you already know what you need to do. It is already swirling in your spirit, and God is waiting for you to walk, to move, to act in obedience to Him. Even now, angels are being assigned to you, to back you up and to open the way for you.

Last year, a concerned mother contacted me because her daughter saw rainbows appearing across her arm. To me, this spoke of promise. The young woman had struggled for many years in her relationship with Jesus Christ, but now He allowed her to see a sign of His promise as a reminder: *"I will never leave you, nor forsake you"* (Hebrews 13:5). God's angels surround us always.

It has been quite a few years now since we first started noticing rainbows appearing. We began having encounters in which angels would show up and rainbows would appear, even in the midst of complete darkness. Sometimes, when we would first see the rainbow light, we would turn the lights off to see what would happen, and the rainbows still appeared.

Sometimes these rainbows will come as one large streak of light. At other times, they look like dancing lights of color appearing all over the room. The founder of the Salvation Army, General William Booth, reported seeing angels robed in brilliant rainbow light. We should also expect to see these angels, more and more!

When we were in the Gold Coast with the lights turned off in our hotel room, a rainbow appeared on the floor. We took a photo of it in the dark. In the natural, that is said to be impossible. You cannot have a rainbow in the dark. I'm not a scientist but from what I understand, a rainbow is a refraction of light into its various colors. Because of that, it is impossible to have a rainbow without light. But God is light, and His angels are messengers who are filled with light. So, we can expect a lot of rainbows to show up, even in dark places.

To me, this is prophetic. God wants to shine forth His light, and He will do so, at times, through the ministry of angels. Expect angels to visit you, bringing a *shift*, even in the darkest moments of your life.

We've had this happen in our home. One night, as we got ready for bed, I turned off all the lights only to notice a rainbow shining on our bathroom door—in the dark! I became so excited that I got Janet out of bed to see it. It was an awesome experience. God speaks to us in these moments, and we thank Him for filling our atmosphere with the presence of His angels.

Speak It Boldly and See It Happen!

When signs and wonders first began happening in our ministry, several preachers said things like, "Brother Joshua, it's wonderful that God is doing such miraculous things in your life but you must only speak about Jesus. Never mention the signs." Because they were older and seemed wiser than me, and because I have always valued the importance of placing Jesus Christ above all else in both word and deed, I heeded these warnings. The problem with their advice, however, was that when we didn't speak about what God was doing, He seemed to do it less. The result was to limit the miracles in our midst.

When God gives us something, He gives it to us in seed form, and with that seed, we are given the responsibility of finding the proper people, places, and atmospheres in which to sow it. God wants us to experience a harvest, but the only way that will happen is if and when we are willing to sow the seed He has given.

Eventually, the Spirit also began speaking to me about the importance of our testimony and our decrees. I saw in the Bible that an angel told John, *"The testimony of Jesus is the spirit of prophecy"* (Revelation 19:10). In other words, if we will be willing to speak about what God has done, we create a door in the spirit world for Him to do it again. Testimonies are essential when working with angels in the glory realm. The more we speak about them, the more we will see them! Knowing this should cause us to come out from under our shells of intimidation and speak openly and often of God's marvels.

One evening, as I spoke about the glory of God, we watched in amazement as angels began to move in our midst. Those in attendance began pointing at something behind me. At that moment, I was standing out on the floor in front of the stage, and when I turned to see what they were pointing at, what I saw amazed me. A large and heavy curtain had been pulled across the stage. It was one of the old-fashioned kind you used to see at movie theaters. It was made of a heavy material, and yet it was swaying back and forth with great intensity. It looked as if there was something or someone behind the curtain, pushing it back and forth violently.

Some of those present didn't consider this to be a supernatural event. They simply assumed that someone was on the stage behind the curtain, pushing it back and forth. When they went up to investigate, they were surprised to find that no one was there. There were no air-conditioning vents blowing that night, and even if there had been, air alone would not have been able to move that heavy curtain as forcefully as it was moving.

The pastors of that church, Ian and Joye Johnson, were filming the whole thing with their video camera. When I went back to New Zealand several years later, they reminded me of that encounter and said they were still amazed by it.

What was it? God was introducing me to the realm of angels, and He gave me that curtain as a visible indicator, something that I and others could witness. Angels were moving in that atmosphere of glory.

Later that night, after the meeting, many people were down on hands and knees picking up hundreds of tiny feathers that had been scattered across the floor. These small tokens of angelic activity were another testimony to the reality of the presence of God's heavenly messengers in our midst.

If you're ready to start *Seeing Angels*, let's pray:

Heavenly Father, thank You for giving me a spirit to perceive the movement of Your angels all around me. As I sense them moving and bringing a shift to my life, I will give You all glory, honor, and praise. I know that You are Lord over all, and that You send these angels to change the atmosphere, as I live in the revelation of an open heaven every day of my life. In Jesus's name, amen!

16

Spiritual Safety and Boundaries

Dear friends, do not believe every spirit,
but test the spirits to see whether they are from God.
1 John 4:1 (NIV)

The Bible give us specific instructions regarding the spiritual beings that surround our lives on a daily basis, and I would be remiss if I did not mention it: *"Do not believe every spirit, but test the spirits...."* We must learn *how* to test the spirits, and then we must *always* test them. Some who go around talking about angels are, in actuality, encountering dark presences. These are not holy angels at all; they are fallen angels, or what we would call an evil spirit.

Evil spirits are spiritual beings that sometimes masquerade as angels of light. The Bible says that even Satan tries to masquerade in this way. (See 2 Corinthians 11:14.) Not every angel you meet is holy, loving, respectful, and kind. God's holy angels are *for* you, while the fallen angels are *against* you, and their intention is to do you harm. Therefore, it is important to properly understand spiritual safety and boundaries so that your experiences with angels will be pleasant, protected, peaceful, and productive.

Keep in mind that only one-third of the angels in heaven fell with Lucifer. That means that two-thirds of them are still working for us—and this is good news. I don't want you to be fearful; there is no need to be frightened. In this book, I've been showing you scriptural principles to help you properly connect with your angels. But the battle between good and evil is real, and that's why we must test every spirit that comes into our presence. How can we test these spirits? It is done primarily through the gift of discerning spirits that I wrote about in chapter 9. There are, however, other indicators.

For instance, just as there are heavenly aromas associated with the presence of angels, likewise, there are foul aromas associated with evil spirits. At times, you may smell them before you see them. One of the common smells associated with their dark activity is much like the stench of human or animal feces. Another aroma is similar to cigarette, cigar, or marijuana smoke.

There are also feelings associated with the presence of evil spirits. For me, it sometimes feels like a big rubber band is being placed around my head. At other times, it feels like a sudden migraine or sharp headache. I'm not saying that those who suffer from frequent migraines or severe headaches are necessarily experiencing the presence of evil spirits, but it is certainly an evil attack, and you need to take authority over it.

The experience I'm talking about happens when everything seems fine, when suddenly, without explanation, a sharp pain hits you, like a tight rubber band is squeezing your head. When this has happened to me, I came to understand that it was an indicator of a dark presence. Those kinds of spirits are not holy, and their purpose is never good or godly. When anything like this happens, take authority over those evil spirits. Use your believer's authority and tell them to go. When you do this, release will come.

Just as there is a heavenly weightiness that comes to us when angels are present (an abundance of joy, peace, blessing, etc.), there is also an ungodly heaviness that sometimes comes on your chest when evil spirits are present. This feeling is not good at all and can be described as being similar to suffocating.

When I was a child, I suffered from occasional bouts of a sudden, paralyzing fear. This needs a little more explanation because the presence of God's holy angels can also cause fear, as we discussed in chapter 12. A response of fear was often recorded in the Scriptures. There is a natural tendency to be afraid of anything that is unfamiliar. Our flesh is uncomfortable with the unfamiliar. When we experience fear, therefore, it is not necessarily an indication of an evil presence. It may well be that our flesh is learning how to deal with something new. What I experienced as a child is different. It was a paralyzing fear, and it was absolutely ungodly. It wasn't just a feeling in the flesh, but a completely overwhelming sensation. If you have not been built up in the Spirit, it can feel as if there is nothing you can do to fight it or escape it. You may feel like you've been captured and bound, with no hope of ever being free. But that's not true!

Children are extremely sensitive to the presence of angels, and they are also sensitive to the presence of evil spirits. As I noted, this paralyzing fear came to me as a child, and the purpose of evil spirits for bringing this on me was an attempt to short-circuit my destiny. Listen to your children when they talk about such encounters. It is very common for children to see things in the night and call to their parents to come into their room. They think they are seeing or feeling the presence of "monsters." As parents, our usual reaction to this is to say, "There's no such thing as monsters. Go back to sleep." Well, that may be true of the kinds of monsters portrayed in Hollywood movies, but there are evil spirits who are certainly monstrous. When we outright dismiss the supernatural, it can have a negative effect on the childlike faith and trust of our loved ones.

I'm not saying that we do this on purpose. Usually, we do it innocently. We present our children with our human reasoning, our natural logic, our understanding, but it is dangerous because it can have the effect of desensitizing children to the spirit world.

What is the proper response to a child's fears? It is to teach them about the reality of the angelic world and to let them know that God's angels surround their life, to protect them from all harm:

> *For he will command his angels concerning you to guard you in all your ways.* (Psalm 91:11 NIV)

Speak this promise over your children and let them learn it for themselves. Assure them that God's holy angels are always with them, watching over them, guarding them at all times and in all places.

That's the right response to give our children. They don't need to be afraid of the terror that comes by night (see verse 5) but can take authority over it. Together, you can thank God for His angels, the heavenly company that surrounds the whole family.

Detecting the Counterfeit

When speaking of evil spirits and their activity, the important thing is that you know what to look for. It's a lot like a banker, looking carefully over the money in his care to ensure that he doesn't accept any suspicious currency that might be counterfeit. In order to recognize fake money, he undergoes good training that includes plenty of experience handling the real thing. Once he is accustomed to the look and feel of authentic currency, it becomes difficult for a counterfeit bill to get past him. He knows the real from the fake. By spending time with the genuine, he learns what is false. Over time, his eye and his touch become extremely sensitive to the counterfeit. He knows what the real looks like, and anything else stands out like Monopoly money to him. To the untrained, fake money looks and feels like the real thing. But to the trained expert, the look and feel is all wrong. Unless you have practiced this enough, you might be easily fooled.

The way in which we grow in our discerning spirits is much the same. Spending more time in the presence of God's glory and focusing on what is authentic will save us from experiencing much grief and tragedy. When we're in the presence of God's holiness, looking upon Jesus Christ, then, when something that is not from Him tries to enter our lives, warning bells go off immediately. Our alarm system begins to ring. Because we know what God is like, what His presence is like, what His Word is like, and what His works are like, we instantly know when it's not Him, and we can take authority over the situation so that we can continue resting and enjoying the atmosphere of divine presence.

Spending time in the atmosphere of the Spirit is spending time in the atmosphere of purity and truth:

> But when he, the Spirit of truth, comes, he will guide you into all the truth. He will not speak on his own; he will speak only what he hears, and he will tell you what is yet to come. (John 16:13 NIV)

Then you will know the truth, and the truth will set you free.

(John 8:32 NIV)

Spending time in the atmosphere of truth, the atmosphere of purity, the atmosphere of faith, the atmosphere of anointing, and the atmosphere of glory trains us in the truth of who God is, and that truth sets us free from any other thing that tries to hinder our walk with the Lord.

Boundary Lines

The dictionary defines a *boundary* as "a line which marks the limits of an area; a dividing line." When speaking about angels, it's important for us to understand God's boundaries and limits for angels in the life of a believer. If we go beyond those limits, we will encounter problems. Therefore, understanding the boundary lines is necessary if you want to remain in safe territory. There is a protection line in the spirit world, and that line is the Word of God.

Mary K. Baxter has shared:

Not all angels are kind and benevolent. There are good angels and there are evil angels. Good angels continually seek to do God's will, and they work for our benefit. Evil angels seek to deceive us about their true intentions toward us. They are demons who want to harm us rather than help us. This is why it can be very dangerous to learn about angels from those who don't have a solid biblical understanding of their true nature and ways.[41]

Although the supernatural world is vast and wide, any spiritual reality outside of God's Word can lead to pain, devastation, and ultimate tragedy. Jesus declared, "*Enter through the narrow gate. For wide is the gate and broad is the road that leads to destruction, and many enter through it. But small is the gate and narrow the road that leads to life, and only a few find it*" (Matthew 7:13–14 NIV). We must remain within the boundaries of God's Word. When we do this, we will also be covered by the protective blood of Jesus and the blessing of the Holy Spirit. Divine angels honor God and His Word.

---

41. Mary K. Baxter, *A Divine Revelation of Angels* (New Kensington, PA: Whitaker House, 2003), 26.

Fallen Angels

Peter informed us that, when certain angels sinned, God *"cast them down to hell, and delivered them into chains of darkness, to be reserved to judgment"* (2 Peter 2:4). In the same manner, Jude stated, *"The angels which kept not their first estate, but left their own habitation, He has reserved in everlasting chains under darkness to the judgment of the great day"* (Jude 1:6), where these angels will suffer *"the vengeance of eternal fire"* (Jude 1:7). Jesus declared that this everlasting fire was *"prepared for the devil and his angels"* (Matthew 25:41).

There is no grace for the fallen angels, and they cannot be redeemed. This is why the holy angels are said to mysteriously desire to look into matters of salvation and redemption. (See 1 Peter 1:10–12.) Only humans can testify to the amazing grace of Christ, as the Holy Spirit reveals it to us. In the same way that *"Satan himself masquerades as an angel of light"* (2 Corinthians 11:14 NIV), these fallen angels, as evil spirits, sometimes attempt to present themselves as good spirits, when in reality, they are foul, dark, and impure.

There are many names used for these fallen angels within the Scriptures. These include:

+ Deaf and mute spirit (Mark 9:25)

+ Spirit of deception (1 Kings 22:21)

+ Spirit of distress (1 Samuel 16:15)

+ Spirit of Egypt (Isaiah 19:3)

+ Spirit of falsehood (Micah 2:11)

+ Spirit of harlotry (Hosea 4:12)

+ Spirit of heaviness (Isaiah 61:3)

+ Spirit of ill-will (Judges 9:23)

+ Spirit of infirmity (sickness) (Luke 13:11)

+ Spirit of lies (1 Kings 22:23)

+ Spirit of perversion (Isaiah 19:14)

+ Spirit of uncleanliness (Zechariah 13:2 and Matthew 12:43)

Do not be deceived by these seducing spirits. You can know a fallen angel by the following traits:

- Fallen angels always lie. God and His angels never lie, but, instead, they lead us into truth.

- Fallen angels will present you with a message that is contrary to God's Word. True angels will direct you to God's Word.

- Fallen angels will draw you to themselves and away from God. Divine angels work for God and will always point you toward seeing Jesus, high and exalted on the throne of your heart.

- Fallen angels will lead you away from a life in the Spirit and corrupt you with a desire for carnal things. God's angels do the opposite.

- Fallen angels carry an uneasy, disturbing, and dark atmosphere with them. You may not always immediately recognize what is wrong but the witness of the Holy Spirit within you will reveal that something is not right. Pure angels bring an atmosphere of peace, calm, and reassurance of God's goodness.

If a fallen angel, as an evil spirit, should appear before you or come to speak to you, you must immediately take authority over it and command it to leave. You have been given this supernatural power in the spirit world.

Boundaries for Angels

Angels work for God and carry out His purposes. But unlike God, angels do have their limits. They are not omnipotent (all-powerful), omnipresent (all-pervasive), or omniscient (all-knowing). Let's take a look in Scripture to see what is permissible and what is not permissible for angels, as they work in our lives.

Angels Do Not Live Inside Us

The Holy Spirit has the only legal spiritual permission to live inside the life of a believer. Although it is possible for God's angels to feed us spiritual food, heavenly scrolls, or other divine impartations, an angel will never come to "live inside of you." It is wrong for any spirit to possess you, except for the abiding presence of the Holy Spirit. That's why we are instructed to "cast out" evil spirits. They are not legally permitted to live inside a human person.

We Do Not Work for Angels

Angels have been assigned by God to work for us. You will never be enslaved by an angel. If you sense that a spiritual being is bossing you around, I can assure you that it is not an angel from God. Your angels have been assigned to your life to work with you and for you. Yes, it's true that they may bring specific directives from heaven for your life, but you will never feel bound by them. The instructions, messages, and revelations angels deliver will enable you to be freer to live the life Christ has called you to live.

Angels Cannot Alter Spiritual Laws

Although it's possible for angels to bend physical laws because they are spiritual beings, they will never alter spiritual laws. Holy angels are not rebellious and they always honor spiritual principles that have been established by God. Sowing and reaping is a spiritual law (see Galatians 6:7), and even angels of abundant provision will not break that law. Instead, they will work to connect you with the flow of spiritual laws so that you can increase and enter into the fullness of God.

Angels Are Not Called to Teach God's Word

That is your responsibility. The Holy Spirit comes to anoint you, fill you, and lead you into all truth. He is the Teacher, and He wants to teach you. As you give yourself to dedicated study and spending time in God's Word, the Holy Spirit will begin to illuminate that Word for you. Although angels can be carriers of God's words and can deliver divine insights and messages to you, it is only the Holy Spirit who can ultimately quicken a revelatory understanding of it.

Comparing the Work of the Holy Spirit to the Work of Angels

In some ways, comparing the work of angels with the work of the Holy Spirit is like comparing apples and oranges. Although they complement each other, they are on two different levels altogether.

First, I want to shift your thoughts for a moment, and I want you to ask yourself a question: Who is the opposite of God? Many people will automatically respond with either Lucifer or Satan, but that's not true. Lucifer was a created heavenly being (see Ezekiel 28:13) and is now a fallen angel who directs an army of demonic forces (see Isaiah 14:12). Lucifer is the exact opposite of God's holy angels. Looking through Scripture, we discover that God has no equal, and therefore, no opposite. He is God. There is no one to compare God to. There is none like Him. The Christian faith is not about a yin-and-yang balance of good and evil. No! God is always good, and He always reigns supreme. As believers, we must learn how to proclaim that Jesus is Lord in every situation and circumstance—because that is the ultimate truth.

As we proceed with this conversation, we must begin by remembering that the Holy Spirit *is* God. He takes first place, and there is no one like Him. However, the Holy Spirit does work in agreement with angels in order to accomplish heavenly assignments on earth. In general, it seems that Holy Spirit ministry begins within us and works itself outward, whereas angelic ministry begins outside us and works itself within. As a believer, it's vital to understand the difference between the work of the Holy Spirit and the working of angels in our lives. To help with this, I have compiled a comparison chart to help you understand this difference:

The Work of the Holy Spirit and the Work of Angels	
THE HOLY SPIRIT	**ANGELS**
Empowers	*Encourage*
Spirit-filled life (Galatians 5:22–25)	**Watch over and direct us to God** (Daniel 4)
Dwells inside us (1 Corinthians 6:19)	**Work beside us** (Luke 4:10)
Produces the born-again experience (John 3:6)	**Align us in order to rejoice with born-again experience** (Luke 15:10)
Holds Wisdom of Universe (1 Peter 1:12)	**Hunger for Wisdom** (1 Peter 1:12)
Communicates directly, Spirit to spirit (Psalm 42:7)	**Serve the Holy Spirit, because He is part of the Godhead** (Hebrews 1:4,6)
He is the Word and He is God (John 1:1)	**Obey the Word as Ministers for God** (Psalm 103:20)
Knows the thoughts and intents of the heart (Jeremiah 17:10, Romans 8:27)	**Know the outward functions and tendencies of mankind** (Psalm 34:7)

The "3-R Test" for All Angel Encounters

1. The Revelation

If an encounter contradicts the revelation of the Word of God, stay clear of it. Everything that angels do will fall perfectly in line and be totally consistent with His Word. All of our spiritual experiences must have their foundations in that Word. (See Isaiah 55:11; Matthew 24:35; John 17:17.)

2. The Recognition

Ask yourself this question: "Who is recognized through this spiritual encounter?" Are your eyes being directed toward the angel or is the angel directing your attention to Jesus and the fulfilment of His plans for your life? Jesus Christ must be glorified through every authentic spiritual experience. If the encounter serves to lower Jesus Christ from His position in the godhead, stay clear of it. (See John 1:1; Romans 16:27.)

3. The Results

What is the resulting fruit of the spiritual encounter? The Bible clearly tells us that good trees produce good fruit. Prophetically speaking, this represents anything that is spiritually grown in our life. The "fruit" of your encounter will reveal the "tree" from which it came. (See Matthew 7:17–20, 12:33.)

Angels are willing and ready to minister. Are you willing and ready to command them? Just do it, and then watch for the signs and atmospheric shifts that follow. Through this book, you've received instruction from the Word that has imparted enough faith for this realm to open fully for you. Now it's time to pay close attention to the movement of angels around you.

Remember, sometimes it may be overt, while at other times it might be subtle. Tune in and really allow your spirit to connect with the Spirit of God. Be watchful everywhere you go. There is no doubt in my mind that as you do, you will begin *Seeing Angels*.

Let's pray:

Heavenly Father, I thank You for angel encounters in my home, in my place of business, and everywhere I go. I thank You for surrounding my life with Your angels of protection, deliverance, and comfort. I can feel their guarding presence around me. I know that Your angels of healing and abundant provision are working right now to bring forth a greater harvest in every area of my life where there has been lack and despair. I trust You, as You have set angels of divine love before me to cover my relationships. You have given me a greater awareness of angels on extraordinary assignment, and for that, I am forever grateful. Thank You for encompassing me with Your angels who watch over my church, city, and nation. You have opened my spirit eyes to discern Your angels who are moving in my life. I have hidden Your Word in my heart, so that as I speak Your truth, the angels will take notice and minister at my command. I ever praise You and give You all glory. May Jesus be magnified in my life forevermore! Amen!

Appendix 1:
Activations for Angel Encounters

N ow that I've shared some of my personal experiences and built a scriptural framework for the work of angels in your life, I want to give you the opportunity to activate this realm. Spiritually activating the Word is a biblical concept. We know that faith without works is dead (see James 2:17) and that Jesus Himself said, *"Anyone who listens to my teaching and follows it is wise"* (Matthew 7:24 NLT). Consider these important verses from James 1:22–25, which encourage us to act on the insight, wisdom, and revelation that we've received from the Scriptures:

> But don't just listen to God's word. You must do what it says. Otherwise, you are only fooling yourselves. For if you listen to the word and don't obey, it is like glancing at your face in a mirror. You see yourself, walk away, and forget what you look like. But if you look carefully into the perfect law that sets you free, and if you do what it says and don't forget what you heard, then God will bless you for doing it.   (NLT)

I would highly encourage you to download a copy of my album *Activating Angels in Your Life*. I know that you will find it extremely beneficial. On those audio tracks, I both speak the Word of God concerning the angels that surround you and allow time for you to experience the manifestation of the words that are being declared. A peaceful atmosphere, anointed instrumental worship music, and specific time set apart for the Lord will afford you the best experience.

In this appendix, you'll find seven activations you can use for angel encounters, but I would only encourage you to practice these after you have finished reading this book in its entirety. The biblical teaching about angels puts everything into proper perspective and lays out appropriate boundaries and guidelines to keep you safe in the process.

I have used these activations in both personal and group settings and I have discovered that they work best when they are approached with an open heart. Do not feel limited by these activations but instead, utilize them to springboard into these realms of angelic presence. Allow Jesus Christ to be Lord of your life and let the Holy Spirit be your guide.

Activation #1: Beginner's Guide to Seeing Angels

I want to give you an activation you can try at home right now. In order to do this, you will need a partner. *It is important that you and your partner are in agreement regarding the concepts I am teaching here.* You can do this in any location, but if you are new to these things, you may want to specifically choose a location that is private, quiet, and conducive to helping you focus spiritually.

Choose which one of you will go first (you will be taking turns). To begin, stand facing each other, about five feet apart. Place your right hand on your heart and pray this prayer with me:

Heavenly Father, I ask for Your Spirit to open the eyes of my heart, that I might begin to see. Help me discern by Your Spirit. I desire to see Your angels so that I can interact with them. I receive this gift of spiritual vision. In Jesus's name, amen!

After you have prayed this prayer, I want you to look at your partner. Instead of focusing on their facial features or physical attributes, I want you to "look through them" and prayerfully begin noticing the forms, shapes, lines, and shadows that appear around and above them. Eventually, you will begin noticing the outline of the angel who stands guard behind them.

Don't feel worried or pressured during this activation; instead, feel the joy and playfulness of God in it. For most people, everything about them will begin to seem translucent. Doing this exercise helps you to practice seeing in the Spirit. If you are determined to ask God for this gift, you must be willing to use what He gives you.

If you don't notice anything at all, it may be because your eyes are being distracted by natural interference. You could ask your partner to stand against a neutral-colored wall to help you to focus with fewer distractions. It may take multiple attempts. For many years now, your eyes have been trained to focus on what is seen, but God wants to teach you how to see with Spirit eyes, how to see what is normally unseen.

Let your partner try this activation as well.

Activation #2: Looking for Detail

Now, I want you to repeat the first activation, but this time, I want you to pray this prayer:

Heavenly Father, I ask for Your Spirit to open the eyes of my heart and bring clarity to my vision. Help me to discern by Your Spirit. I desire to see Your angels so that I can interact with them. I receive this gift of spiritual clarity. In Jesus's name, amen!

Once you begin noticing forms and outlines around your partner, I want you to press in with your spiritual eyes to see colorful formations and lights, details of angelic wardrobe, including a sword, trumpet, book, or other object the angel may be holding. Begin to notice whether or not this angel has wings. Can you tell if the angel is appearing in male or female form? As you notice such details, even if they are blurry at first, speak out what you are noticing. Don't be afraid. Say what you are seeing in the spirit realm, as things become clearer to you.

Let your partner try this too.

Activation #3: Asking Your Angel's Name

Once you begin noticing signs of angelic movement in your life, it will build your confidence to ask questions. When you feel ready, in a quiet but audible voice, ask your angel, "What is your name?" The response can come in several different ways but, again, don't feel rushed.

Here are some of the ways your answer might come:

+ You may notice, over the next several days, that your eyes continue to be drawn to the same word over and over. This could be your angel directing you to "see" the name. You will know for sure by the inner witness of the Holy Spirit, confirming this name to you.

+ You may sense a specific name or word in your heart when you have asked. This is the inner voice of the Holy Spirit speaking to you, confirming the name of your angel.

+ You may hear a gentle whisper in your ear. This is your angel speaking directly to you. When you hear the name, respond by saying, "Thank you, I'm glad that God has sent you to help me."

+ You may suddenly "think" the name as it pops into your mind, or you may see a picture that somehow reveals the name—this can include words, a loved one with the same name, an object, etc.

Activation #4: Steps for Engaging with Angels of Healing

Physical healing and emotional healing come in the same way. As you follow these spiritual steps, you will make room for God's healing angels to come and minister to you:

1. You Must Believe God's Word Regarding Healing

God's Word is His will. What He says He really means. Search the Scriptures and find out what God says about divine healing. Here are some good passages to start with:

+ Exodus 23:25

+ Psalm 107:20

+ Isaiah 53:5

+ Isaiah 58:8

+ Matthew 4:23

+ Matthew 14:14

Once you discover the truths put forth in these passages, begin to speak them over your life. As you hear God's healing Word, it will become life to you and bring a fresh infusion of faith to believe Him for the miracle you need.

I have recorded an album called *Receive Your Healing*.[42] Many people have reported receiving healing miracles as they listened to the spoken Word of God through the anointing on that album. It is filled with both healing Scriptures and prophetic declarations that will grow your faith and plant miracle seeds in your spirit.

2. You Must Accept God's Word for Your Life

The Scriptures remind us that God's Word is forever settled in heaven (see Psalm 119:89), but you must be willing to allow that Word to be settled in *you*. Stop confessing and speaking negative things over your body, mind, and emotions. Your words are filled with both positive and negative power, depending on the words you speak. (See Proverbs 18:21.) As you accept God's healing Word, begin speaking it over yourself. You will soon discover that it is no longer a mechanical action of your mind but, rather, a reflexive habit that naturally flows from your heart.

God's Word will change you. God's Word will transform your life. God's Word will position you for miracles. God's Word will increase your ability to receive everything He has for you. As the Scriptures say,

> Pay attention to what I say; turn your ear to my words. Do not let them out of your sight, keep them within your heart; for they are life to those who find them and health to one's whole body.
>
> (Proverbs 4:20–22 NIV)

3. You Must Forgive Yourself and Others

Unforgiveness can be the largest stumbling block to receiving the healing you need. The Scriptures remind us: "*If you forgive other people when they sin against you, your heavenly Father will also forgive you*" (Matthew 6:14 NIV). Unforgiveness is a lie. It doesn't make you better; it only makes you bitter. Unforgiveness only hurts the one who holds on to it. There is a great quote about resentment, often attributed to Nelson Mandela, that I believe

---

42. Joshua Mills and Steve Swanson, *Receive Your Healing*, available as a digital download or physical CD at joshuamills.com.

works just as well for unforgiveness: "Unforgiveness is the poison we drink, hoping that someone else will die."

You must learn to forgive others for their wrong-doings and personal offenses against you. This doesn't justify what they've done—they will one day answer to God for their own actions—but it releases you from being shackled to that situation. This is a big step toward complete healing.

You must also learn to forgive yourself, and sometimes this can be the most difficult part of the process. You must forgive your body for the pain it has caused you, you must forgive your mind for the emotional torment you have suffered, and you must forgive yourself for procrastinating and allowing sickness to continue to exist. Ask God to show you the areas of your life in which you need to release forgiveness. As the Lord shows these things to you, you can say a simple prayer:

> Lord, help me to forgive _____. I release this situation into Your hands, and I ask for Your healing angels to carry sickness away from me, in Jesus's name.

You may need to pray this prayer a few times. But the more you ask God for His help and allow His angels to intervene, the more you will feel His peace over the situation, until you can finally say:

> Lord, I completely forgive _____. Thank You for healing me. I receive Your miracle touch, in Jesus's name.

As you take actions toward healing, turning away from the evil of unforgiveness, Scripture promises: "*This will bring health to your body and nourishment to your bones*" (Proverbs 3:8 NIV).

4. You Must Act on Your Healing

The final step toward receiving your healing is to act upon the Word that you believe and have accepted it as final truth in your life. James 2:17 reminds us: "*Even so faith, if it has not works, is dead, being alone.*" That word *works* means "action." Your forgiveness of others and of yourself will position you to take action and step into a new healing realm. You can be sure that the healing angels are there to help you enter into it as well. Just as the sick and diseased in biblical days would be given the opportunity to step into the angelically-stirred healing waters of the pool of Bethesda, as you take a step and move into action toward your healing, you will discover those healing waters opening up within your own personal life.

Every action causes a reaction, and every action of faith causes a reaction of miracles. When the woman with the issue of blood pressed through the crowd and reached out to touch the hem of Christ's garment, healing virtue was released to her. (See Mark 5:25–29.) After hearing Jesus's specific instructions, the ten lepers obeyed, and as they went, they were cleansed of their disease. (See Luke 17:11–14.) The centurion had faith to ask Jesus to heal his servant, and the miracle happened as he journeyed home due to the soldier's complete trust in the authority of Christ's healing word. (See Matthew 8:13.) Take action toward your healing today and begin *Seeing Angels* ministering healing to you.

Activation #5: Steps for Engaging with Angels of Abundant Provision

There are steps you can begin taking now to activate angels of provision in your life. Are you ready to begin seeing a change in your financial situation? Are you ready for overflowing blessing, supernatural replenishment, and divine abundance to flow in your life?

I've spoken about the many different ways in which angels can come to us. One of the most important things to remember is that God doesn't send angels into your life to take over responsibilities He has given specifically to you. Angels are ministering spirits, sent to assist every believer in fulfilling the call of God upon their lives. In other words, you can't become lazy and decide that you will now sit back and let angels do everything to provide for you. That's not the way it works, and that would be foolish.

The Scriptures tell us that God opens the heavens to bless the works of *your hand.* (See Deuteronomy 28:12.) You have to put your hand to work. As you set out to do all that God has called you to do, and as you begin to put these principles into action, you can expect heaven to open, and supernatural support to come, as angels of provision begin working alongside you to ensure that you are fully blessed.

Here are three main areas that will help you cooperate with your angels of provision:

1. Be Thankful

Exchange any words and feelings of resentment for an attitude of gratitude. This will change everything for you. Many years ago, I remember driving to a ministry appointment with another minister friend. On our way to the church, I had to stop to fill up the car with gas. Overnight, it seemed that gas prices had skyrocketed, and I began complaining. "I can't believe how high these prices are! How do they ever expect people to pay this much for gasoline? Do they think money just grows on trees?"

I was expecting my friend to join me in my complaining but, instead, he kindly but firmly answered, "Joshua, you can be thankful that God has provided money for your gas, and He always will." That one sentence changed everything for me, and I've never forgotten it. No matter what situation we find ourselves in, God has made a way of provision for us. So, instead of complaining, we can begin rejoicing.

Janet has taught people all over the world about the power of spoken words. This has resulted in people changing both the way they think and the way they speak. In response, we have received many testimonies about how people have improved their finances, secured abundant blessings, and enriched many other areas of their lives, simply by changing the words they speak.

God listens to your words (see Psalm 55:17), and angels respond to your words (see Daniel 10:12). Therefore, we must learn to transform our stressing into blessing. Now, when I write a check to pay a bill, I also write "Thank You" in the memo line. I do the same if I'm sending a money transfer online. I know this is unusual—and some might think, *Why should I be thankful that I have to pay bills?* I give thanks because regardless of how things look in the natural, in the glory, I know that there is abundance to pay all my bills. Giving thanks helps me to recognize my blessings, it opens doors of plenty in the Spirit, and it allows me to sense the movement of God's angels of provision in my daily life. When *you* become thankful, the same things will happen in your life.

Psalm 100:4 declares: *"Enter into His gates with thanksgiving, and into His courts with praise: be thankful to Him, and bless His name."* I believe that the supernatural doors that open through our giving thanks allow new angels of provision to enter our lives in plenitude. When we bless the Lord, we're surrounded with heavenly hosts that do the same.

There are many ways we can begin taking action toward being thankful, and each thankful action will cause an angelic reaction. Take some time today to write a meaningful thank-you note to someone. It doesn't need to be long, just make sure it comes from your heart. Try to say "thank you" as often as possible and watch the reaction of others. Guard your words today, and when you notice yourself starting to complain, find a reason to give thanks instead. Then, notice how you begin to feel and how the atmosphere begins to shift when you live with a thankful attitude.

2. Be Generous

Your attitude of gratitude will be sealed through your actions of generosity. The two are connected. The truth is, whatever you're thankful for, you'll be willing to bless. The Scriptures clearly tell us: *"Be you doers of the word, and not hearers only"* (James 1:22), and *"faith without works is dead"* (James 2:20).

Actively begin looking for opportunities to show generosity toward others. This act alone will release you from feeling helpless about your current financial situation and release angels of provision around you. Look at what the Bible says about giving generously:

> *Give, and it shall be given to you; good measure, pressed down, and shaken together, and running over, shall men give into your bosom. For with the same measure that you mete withal it shall be measured to you again.* (Luke 6:38)

When an angel appeared to Cornelius in a supernatural visitation, he provided an important revelatory insight when he said: *"Your prayers and gifts of charity have ascended as a memorial offering before God [an offering made in remembrance of His past blessings]"* (Acts 10:4 AMP). Angels respond to your generosity, and when you begin putting the principles of this chapter into action, you will also begin to see a change in your current situation.

Expect angels to intervene, but don't expect them to do something that is possible for you to do. Your obedience to follow God's instruction permits the angels to cooperate with you, to bring greater results than you could produce in your own strength and ability.

3. Be Willing to Receive

And as soon as the grain is ready, the farmer comes and harvests it with a sickle, for the harvest time has come. (Mark 4:29 NLT)

In terms of scriptural truth, a generous giver has the spiritual right to become a generous receiver. (See 2 Corinthians 9:6.) Actually, it is the responsibility of the one who sows to also make sure that the crop is reaped when harvest time rolls around. What you give in faith will bring a return, but you must also be willing to use your faith to receive the corresponding harvest. This is a biblical principle. (See Galatians 6:9.) No farmer goes into his field planting a seed, expecting that the harvest will magically appear on his front doorstep. That would be foolish. Sometimes it takes bold faith to give, but it also takes bold faith to receive. (See Ephesians 3:12.)

When we are sowing to the heavens, we must believe that something is being activated on our behalf. And if we truly believe that a financial harvest is being created for us, it then becomes our responsibility to command the angels of provision to gather that harvest for us. The Bible shows us that the farmer comes and *"harvests it with a sickle."* Spiritually speaking, that sickle is the prophetic word of God that is spoken from our lips. Remember, the Scriptures declare: *"For the word of God is quick, and powerful, and sharper than any two-edged sword, piercing even to the dividing asunder of soul and spirit, and of the joints and marrow, and is a discerner of the thoughts and intents of the heart"* (Hebrews 4:12). God's Word, as a sickle, must be both believed and decreed.

When God began teaching Rev. Kenneth E. Hagin about exercising the believer's authority regarding finances, He taught him the importance of commanding the spiritual beings that surrounded his life. This included speaking commands to both demonic forces and God's heavenly angels. In his book, *The Midas Touch*, Hagin related this story:

The Lord said to me, "Don't pray about money like you have been. Whatever you need, claim it in Jesus' name. Then say, 'Satan, take your hands off my money.' And then say, 'Go, ministering spirits, and cause the money to come.'"[43]

There would be no point in commanding a harvest to come forth if the seed has not yet been planted, but if you have seed that's been sown, then you can be guaranteed that a harvest is being grown. (See Galatians 6:7.) Many believers have complained about their lack. They've become very good at blaming the devil and commanding demons, casting them out, and taking authority over them. But I think it's much more important to learn how to exercise our believers' authority over angels instead! Angels will begin to move when you command them to do so. (See Matthew 18:18.) Angels of provision are just waiting for your Spirit-directed instructions.

There are realms of divine prosperity that are overtaking you. There is unexpected, uncommon, and extravagant favor filling your life with good things. There is an encounter of prosperity as the cloud of God's glory rolls in upon you. The prosperity of God is rolling in with it, and there is favor on your business and favor on your personal life. God wants to cancel and forgive debts, to turn over properties, homes, and vehicles, and meet other unusual needs. You can have as much of God as you're willing to drink in, as much of Him as you're willing to receive, as much as you're ready to contain. Just take what you need; it's there for the asking.

God is giving us a prosperity anointing. If you have a business and you want it to prosper, press into this anointing. You may be struggling, perhaps others may have spoken doom over your business, but it doesn't matter what bankers say or what any other person says. What matters is what God says, and He says that He wants you to prosper. Your prosperity delights Him.

Get ready to have God cancel some debts for you. Some loans are being forgiven. He is doing this for His glory because He wants His name to be lifted high, not just in the church but also in the world.

---

43. Kenneth E. Hagin, *The Midas Touch: A Balanced Approach to Biblical Prosperity* (Tulsa, OK: Faith Library Publications, 2002), 31.

Activation #6: Steps for Engaging with Angels to Find True Love

There are some things that you can begin to do, even today, to find true and lasting love in your life. Of course, prayer is one of the best ways to get your angels activated (and we will pray together at the end of this appendix), but there are also some other practical keys I want to give you for partnering with the angels of divine love in your life.

1. You Must Start Fresh

Seek healing from God for any past issues, emotional trauma, or anything else that has tried to block loving relationships from coming into your life. Ask God to send His healing angels to minister to you in these areas of need. In the same way that you would not want to find yourself in an intimate relationship with someone who is carrying around a lot of excess baggage from past relationships, you need to make sure that *your* slate is clean and ready for a fresh start.

Although you may have a lot of "life experience" behind you and some disappointing relationships in the past, remember that God sits on the throne, and He says, *"Behold, I make all things new"* (Revelation 21:5). Let Him make things new *for* you and *in* you today.

2. Know Who You're Looking For

Ask yourself this question: "What do I want in a partner?" Think about this and begin to write down your immediate thoughts. Your heart knows what it wants, and the Spirit of God within you will speak to you about what is important. Be specific and identify the physical, emotional, and spiritual qualities you would like to find in a life-long companion.

It's almost impossible to know if the angels of divine love are leading you to the right person if you haven't taken the time to identify the type of person you would like to find. Sometimes that person may be right in front of you and you just haven't noticed them, perhaps because you were too preoccupied thinking about yourself! You might even want to consider making a "husband" or "wife" vision board.

Some years ago, a single friend came to visit us. One morning, he came excitedly out of the guest bedroom and exclaimed, "I had a dream about my wife last night!"

I said, "Oh, wow! That's amazing! What was she like?"

He began to describe the exact details of everything he had seen, even down to her personality. He seemed to be so pleased with this "girl of his dreams." I told him to write it all down because he could use that vision to recognize her once she manifested in his life. Sure enough, several years later, our friend was doing mission work and he found this dream girl in Africa. They are now married and have a small child, and they have made quite a beautiful family.

God wants to do this same thing for you. The angels of divine love are ready to help you, but you have to know who you're looking for.

3. Be Open to Receive Love

Finally, you must be open in order to discover love. Love cannot enter through a closed heart. Often, the reason people are closed to the thought of a new relationship is because of some past hurt or worries that something will go wrong. These feelings come from a place of fear, and they will often cause you to speak your fears out loud. You may have been guilty of worriedly confessing:

"I'm afraid I'll never get married!"

"I don't think anybody ever notices me!"

"Why am I the only one of my friends without a spouse?"

The problem is that your spoken fears are creating the very outcome that you don't want! Stress and worry pull you away from living a life of peace and ease in God.

Know this: You are loved by God. That's why He wants to fill you with His love. Until you receive His love completely, you won't be able to fully love yourself. And, until you can fully love yourself, you won't be able to properly love others. God's love will help you to love yourself—in spite of your personal faults and failures.

The angels of divine love come from the presence of God, and He is the essence of all love, so I believe they carry the gift of divine love with them. This is a perfect love that casts out all fear. (See 1 John 4:18.) His love for you expands your capacity to open up and receive all that God is bringing to you. When you receive God's love and, in turn, begin to love yourself, this becomes highly attractive to others.

Activation #7: The Power of Loosing Angels

Under the New Covenant, Jesus has instructed us: *"Verily I say to you, Whatsoever you shall bind on earth shall be bound in heaven: and whatsoever you shall loose on earth shall be loosed in heaven"* (Matthew 18:18). Having read the part of that Scripture about binding, many believers have become very good at binding the works of the enemy, and that's an important part of our job as Christians. We must take authority over the works and workers of darkness. But the other part of that verse is just as important as the first part. It says: *"whatsoever you shall loose on earth shall be loosed in heaven."* What are we supposed to loose on earth? Angels! God has given us this privilege, and as we've already discussed, the way to do this is through our voice commands.

Look at Revelation 9:14. It says that a voice spoke to the sixth angel, saying, *"Loose the four angels which are bound in the great river Euphrates."* If you continue reading, you will discover that once the voice spoke, the angels were loosed. This, then, is part of the believer's authority in Christ Jesus.

There are many millions of angels awaiting your God-given instruction:

A river of fire was pouring out, flowing from his presence. Millions of angels ministered to him; many millions stood to attend him. Then the court began its session, and the books were opened. (Daniel 7:10 NLT)

Among these millions of angels are some who will guard you (see Psalm 91:11–12), some who will provide for you (see 1 Kings 19:5–8), some who will rescue you (see Acts 12:7), some who will warn you (see Matthew 2:13), some who will strengthen you (see Luke 22:43), and some who will minister to you (see Hebrews 1:14). There are no limits in the glory. Seek the Lord for His will and His Word and begin commanding angels today!

- Command angels to minister to your personal needs. Say: "In the name of Jesus, go forth, ministering spirits, and minister to _____ (name the need in your life)."

- Command angels to minister in your home. Say: "In the name of Jesus, go forth, ministering spirits, and minister to _____ (name the need in your home)."

- Command angels to minister to your family. Say: "In the name of Jesus, go forth, ministering spirits, and minister to _____ (name a family member)."

- Command angels to minister in regard to your finances. Say: "In the name of Jesus, go forth, ministering spirits, and minister to _____ (name a financial situation)."

- Command angels to minister in your church. Say: "In the name of Jesus, go forth, ministering spirits, and minister to _____ (name your church or ministry)."

Appendix II: Angels in the Bible

394 Scripture References

There are thirty-five books of the Bible that are filled with information, insight, and guidance regarding angels and their ministry assignments in heaven and on the earth. This appendix lists all of the Bible verses that reference angels. Use them to strengthen your understanding of angels through studying the Word of God.

ANGEL (used 215 times)

Genesis 16:7–9, 11

Genesis 19:21

Genesis 21:17

Genesis 22:11–12, 15

Genesis 24:7, 40

Genesis 31:11–12

Genesis 48:16

Exodus 3:2

Exodus 12:23

Exodus 14:19

Exodus 23:20, 23

Exodus 32:34

Exodus 33:2

Numbers 20:16

Numbers 22:22–27, 31–32, 34–35

Judges 2:1, 4

Judges 5:23

Judges 6:11–12, 19–22

Judges 13:3, 9, 13, 15–18, 20–21

1 Samuel 29:9

2 Samuel 14:17, 20

2 Samuel 19:27

2 Samuel 24:16–17

1 Kings 13:18

1 Kings 19:5, 7

2 Kings 1:3, 15

2 Kings 19:35

1 Chronicles 21:12, 15–16, 18, 20, 27, 30

2 Chronicles 32:21

Job 33:23

Psalm 34:7

Psalm 35:5–6

Psalm 89:6

Isaiah 37:36

Daniel 3:28

Daniel 6:22

Hosea 12:4

Zechariah 1:9, 11–14, 19–21

Zechariah 2:3–4

Zechariah 3:1, 3–6

Zechariah 4:1, 4–5, 11

Zechariah 5:2, 5, 8, 10

Zechariah 6:4–5

Zechariah 12:8

Matthew 1:20, 24

Matthew 2:13, 19–20

Matthew 28:2, 5, 8

Mark 16:6

Luke 1:11, 13, 18–19, 26, 29–30, 34–35, 38

Luke 2:9, 10, 13, 17, 20–21

Luke 22:43

John 12:29

Acts 5:19

Acts 6:15

Acts 7:30, 35, 38

Acts 8:26

Acts 10:3–4, 7, 22

Acts 11:13

Acts 12:7–11, 15, 23

Acts 23:9

Acts 27:23

1 Corinthians 10:10

2 Corinthians 11:14

Galatians 1:8

Galatians 4:14

Hebrews 1:5

Hebrews 11:28

Revelation 1:1

Revelation 2:1, 8, 12, 18

Revelation 3:1, 7, 14

Revelation 5:2

Revelation 7:2

Revelation 8:3–5, 7–8, 10, 12

Revelation 9:1, 11, 13–14

Revelation 10:1, 5, 7–10

Revelation 11:15

Revelation 14:6, 8–9, 15, 17–19

Revelation 16:2–5, 8, 10, 12, 17

Revelation 17:3, 7, 15

Revelation 18:1, 21

Revelation 19:9, 17

Revelation 20:1, 3

Revelation 21:15, 17

Revelation 22:1, 6, 8, 16

ANGELIC (used 4 times)

2 Samuel 22:11

Psalm 18:10

Psalm 89:7

Ezekiel 28:14

ANGELS (used 108 times)

Genesis 19:1, 10, 12, 15–17

Genesis 28:12

Genesis 32:1, 43

Judges 13:6

Nehemiah 9:6

Job 4:18

Job 5:1

Job 15:15

Job 33:22

Job 38:7

Psalm 78:25, 49

Psalm 89:5

Psalm 91:11

Psalm 103:20–21

Psalm 148:2

Daniel 4:35

Daniel 7:10

Matthew 4:6, 11

Matthew 13:39, 41–42, 49

Matthew 16:27

Matthew 18:10

Matthew 22:30

Matthew 24:31, 36

Matthew 25:31

Matthew 26:53

Mark 1:13

Mark 8:38

Mark 12:25

Mark 13:27

Mark 13:32

Luke 2:15

Luke 4:10

Luke 9:26

Luke 12:8–9

Luke 15:10

Luke 16:22

Luke 20:36

Luke 24:23

John 1:51

John 20:12–13

Acts 7:53

Acts 23:8

Romans 8:38

1 Corinthians 4:9

1 Corinthians 6:3

1 Corinthians 11:10

1 Corinthians 13:1

Galatians 3:19

Colossians 2:18

2 Thessalonians 1:7

1 Timothy 3:16

1 Timothy 5:21

Hebrews 1:4, 6–7, 13–14

Hebrews 2:2, 5, 7, 9, 16

Hebrews 12:22

Hebrews 13:2

1 Peter 1:12

1 Peter 3:22

2 Peter 2:4

2 Peter 2:11

Jude 1:6, 9

Revelation 1:20

Revelation 3:5

Revelation 5:11

Revelation 7:1–2, 11

Revelation 8:2, 6, 13

Revelation 9:14–15

Revelation 12:7–9

Revelation 14:10

Revelation 15:1, 6–8

Revelation 16:1

Revelation 17:1

Revelation 21:9, 12

ARMIES OF HEAVEN *(used 5 times)*

1 Kings 22:19

2 Chronicles 18:18

Psalm 148:2 (* repeat verse)

Luke 2:13 (* repeat verse)

Revelation 19:14

CHERUBIM *(used 62 times)*

Genesis 3:24

Exodus 25:18–20, 22

Exodus 26:1, 31

Exodus 36:8, 35

Exodus 37:7–9

Numbers 7:89

1 Samuel 4:4

2 Samuel 6:2

1 Kings 6:23–25, 29, 32, 35

1 Kings 7:29, 36

1 Kings 8:6–7

2 Kings 19:15

1 Chronicles 13:6

1 Chronicles 28:18

2 Chronicles 3:7, 10–11, 13–14

2 Chronicles 5:7–8

Psalm 80:1

Psalm 99:1

Isaiah 37:16

Ezekiel 9:3

Ezekiel 10:1–9, 11–12, 14–20

Ezekiel 11:22

Ezekiel 41:8, 25

Hebrews 9:5

SERAPHIM (used 2 times)
Isaiah 6:2, 6

About the Author

Joshua Mills is an internationally recognized ordained minister of the gospel, as well as a recording artist, keynote conference speaker, and author of more than twenty books and spiritual training manuals. His most recent book with Whitaker House was *Moving in Glory Realms*. He is well known for his unique insights into the glory realm, prophetic sound, and the supernatural atmosphere that he carries. For more than twenty years, he has helped people discover the life-shifting truth of salvation, healing, and deliverance for spirit, soul and body. Joshua and his wife, Janet, co-founded International Glory Ministries, and have ministered on six continents in over seventy-five nations around the world. Featured in several film documentaries and print articles, including *Charisma* and *Worship Leader Magazine*, together, they have ministered to millions around the world through radio, television, and online webcasts, including appearances on TBN, Daystar, GodTV, *It's Supernatural! with Sid Roth*, *100 Huntley Street*, and *Everlasting Love* with Patricia King. Their ministry is located in both Palm Springs, California, and London, Ontario, Canada, where they live with their three children: Lincoln, Liberty, and Legacy.